LONELY IN BUSINESS

AND WHY YOU DON'T HAVE TO BE

JOSH PHEGAN

Copyright © 2017 Josh Phegan

All rights reserved.

ISBN: 1548414891
ISBN-13: 978-1548414894

DEDICATION

To you. I've written this for you because you matter and you have everything you need to have a much bigger future than your past. You don't have to be lonely in business any longer.

"Your business life should be nothing but a daring adventure, where you bite off more than you can chew, through an energetic and audacious vision, that forces you to new levels, in figuring out how to get the best people on ground working highly effective systems, to deliver exceptional experiences that turn customers into raving evangelists."
– Josh Phegan

JOSH PHEGAN

FOREWORD

It is totally unsurprising that Josh has succeeded in detailing his life's lessons and teachings into a book of practical perfection.

In some ways the book is an extension of his on-stage coaching, into a tangible resource of "success insurance", delivered with trademark bulletproof confidence and a marksman's precision.

But it also a much deeper extension of his own self; a raw deconstruction of a life's journey; honest; intimate; inspirational; a story of what lies beneath his towering success, from blueprint to strong foundations.

I first met Josh in 2000. We shared the roof of an employer, a great local and independent family-owned newspaper in Albury-Wodonga called The Border Mail.

Josh had an incredible energy and capacity to listen, challenge and learn. It was obvious to all that neither the building nor the region would satisfy his ambition for long.

His star wasn't just on the rise. He was simply in another universe.

And so years later as an international star of the real estate industry, a coach to many in Australia, New Zealand, the UK, US and UAE, speaking at more than 200 live events a year, Josh now for the first time looks back in detail on his own journey as a part of looking forward to yours.

I doubt anyone will read this book and not be better placed to plot their course to greater success.

This is Josh's commitment: to create three forms of fitness – mental, physical and financial - for anyone prepared to invest in a relationship.

He will support you at every step with systems and structures; how to begin, grow capacity, hook on to a much bigger future, scale your growth, bring other people on to the team and fulfil potential we are all born with.

You will never be lonely in business if this book sits within your reach.

Simon Dulhunty,

Former Editor The Border Mail (Albury-Wodonga)
Former Editor The Illawarra Mercury (Wollongong)
Former Editor The Sun-Herald (Sydney)
Former GM Mobile, Fairfax Media (The Sydney Morning Herald, The Age, The Australian Financial Review)

Current:

Non Executive Director, TopBetta Holdings Ltd (ASX: TBH)
Chairman, The Kennedy Foundation (Australia)
Board member, Australian Chinese Primary Industry Council (ACPIC)
Board member, Paga Hill Development Company (Papua New Guinea)
Board member, Centenary Institute foundation committee
Private Media Adviser to international, national corporates and individuals.

CONTENTS

PART 1: FITNESS

1. Instill A Dream Page 9
2. Coming In To Land, Just Before Taking Off Page 11
3. $400 An Hour Page 13
4. Broken Windows And No Video Page 17
5. Mediocre Dreams And Big Dreams Take The Same Amount Of Effort – Larry Page Page 19
6. Business Is The Ultimate Sport – Mark Cuban Page 21
7. If You Don't Make The Decision to F!*king Back Yourself In, Who Will? – David Brown Page 23
8. Your Biggest Challenge Is That You'll Never Be Successful Because You've Just Got Your Toe In The Water; If You Dive In You Might Be A Fighting Chance – Chris Jones Page 25
9. What Drives You? Page 27
10. Live A Life You'd re-live. Goals Matter Page 29
11. The Questions You Ask And The Answers You Give Page 31
12. We Are Young To The Degree That Out Ambition Is Greater Than Our Memories Page 33
13. The Truth Page 35
14. Fitness Just Isn't Physical Page 37
15. Fitness Over Sickness. Irontribe. Page 39
16. Mental Energy Matters Page 43
17. When Anxiety, Insecurity And Lack Of Confidence Take You Out Page 47
18. Have An Inner Scorecard For Success And Don't Care What Anyone Else Ever Says – Warren Buffet Page 49
19. It's Not The Words That You Use, It's How You Make People Feel That Matters Page 53
20. Values Matter Page 55
21. The Five Values Of The Josh Phegan Company Page 57
22. Business Fitness Matters Page 61
23. Business Rules For Expansion Will Set You Free Page 65
24. Who Pays The Bills Page 67
25. Financial Fitness Is A Resource and Resources Bring Choices And Give You The Fuel To Achieve Your Potential Page 69
26. True Net Wealth Matters Page 71
27. Relationship Fitness Page 73
28. Business Matters Page 77
29. Recovery Is The Key To Keeping Fresh Page 79
30. Productivity Hacks Page 81
31. If You Are Going To Use It, You Need To Be Effective Page 85
32. Consistency Matters Page 87

33. The Competitor Doesn't Pay The Bills Page 89
34. Why Do Feelings Matter? Let's Just Do The Deal Page 91
35. Who You Are Becoming Is Much More Important Than Who You Are Page 93
36. Discipline And Persistence Page 95

PART 2: THE PEOPLE

37. The Consigliere Page 97
38. The Mastermind Page 99
39. Tormentors Page 101
40. Keeping Balanced Page 103
41. Polarity Page 105
42. Family Page 107

PART 3: SYSTEMS

43. Getting Consistent Results Page 109
44. You Have To Grow Page 115
45. Results. If It Doesn't Matter Who Wins Or Loses, Then Why Do They Keep Score? – Vince Lombardi Page 117
46. Find A Way Page 119
47. A Little History Worth Repeating: The Secret To Building A Winning Team Page 121
48. Letting Go Is Teaching People How To Grow Page 125
49. 10 Key Skills And Why Your Approach Matters Page 127
50. Make It Easy On Yourself Page 131
51. Career Progression Page 133
52. Clarity On What Matters – The Big Three Page 135
53. Prospecting At Its Best Page 137
54. How Referrals Work Page 139
55. No, Really, How Does It Feel Page 141
56. How Fat Is Your Database? Page 143
57. Language Matters Page 145
58. 80%, Ship It Page 147
59. Meet Andrew Page 149
60. Simple Productivity Hacks That Change The Game Page 153
61. Show Me Your Calendar, Your Bank Statement And Your Mobile Phone And I'll Tell You Your Priorities Page 155
62. Superman Versus Super Team – The Bigger The Dream The More Important The Team Page 159
63. Eliminate Distractions Page 161
64. Basics & Extras Page 163
65. Build Your Motor Page 165
66. If You Met Yourself From 10 Years Ago, What Would Your Advice Be To Yourself From 10 Years Ago? Page 167
67. The Creed Page 169
68. The Cycle Of Completion Page 171
69. The Final Chapter … For Now Page 173

PART 1: FITNESS.

CHAPTER 1: INSTIL A DREAM.

You miss 100% of the shots you don't take. Wayne Gretzky.

The most important thing you can do as a parent is to instil a dream in your children and then help them to achieve it.

It was 1988 and my Mum and Dad had had a rare but heated argument, because my Dad wasn't spending enough time with the kids. So Dad's solution was to take them to work. So there I was heading out to help my Dad sell houses in a small country town in regional Australia.

As a six-year-old, I was shy and quiet, but I would watch and listen to everything I could. I have memories of my Dad waking very early to use what he called the 'golden hour' to improve himself. It's where he'd do all of his studying to become an even better version of himself.

As we jumped in the car together, the young child that left the house that day was not the same as the one that returned. My dad's first routine was to take the cassette tape from the packaging and place it into the player. The car was better known to him as the 'university on wheels.' And with that, a booming voice took over the conversation. "I'm Zig Ziglar and I wanna see you and I mean you at the top".

Dad would over the next few years recount a story to me of how one day he went to the big smoke to a conference, where he was standing out the front. Then a large car rolled up; it was the longest car he'd ever seen. It went and went and went until finally, the car came to a grinding halt and a guy jumps out the back, looks Dad straight in the eye and says "I'm Zig Ziglar and I wanna see you and I mean you at the top".

Dad had met Zig. Imagine being that guy that would walk into the conference from your chauffeured limousine, with 1000s of people in the crowd, with their pens and paper ready to take the notes that would help them to achieve their potential, learning from the lessons. And with that, the dream had begun; imagine if one day, you too could be just like Zig?

CHAPTER 2: COMING IN TO LAND, JUST BEFORE TAKING OFF.

There I was coming in to land in Queenstown, New Zealand. The 24 hours before that had been the worst I'd ever experienced. An off-the-charts competitor was going AWOL on me. He'd lost it because of what we were doing as a company as, one by one, customers were turning to the alternative — I was that alternative.

Naive in business, I was shaken to my very core. Threatening calls, emails, SMSs and a barrage of accusations in under 24 hours had left me motionless. My body had been drained of any energy to live, my mind was mush and I wasn't thinking straight. I was in a tailspin of fear and so much so that I was shaking, sweating and so nervous I couldn't string any words together.

The fear had gotten to me so much that I just could not see a way forward; this guy had convinced me that if I dared even mention the word real estate, I'd be sued and everything I'd ever worked for would be taken away. All my strength and business nous were destroyed. Everything I'd ever worked for was blown up in seconds. I couldn't do it. I couldn't even imagine going to the office. I was convinced that if I did that, I'd find the letter from the lawyers and life as I knew it would be over.

I rang my assistant at the time and drove straight to her house. There I sat with her and her boyfriend, an absolute mess. I was crying, visibly shaking, sweating up a storm and unable to move. I was owned by something that wasn't even real.

After leaving that house that night, I called the one person in the world who I thought could help, a little-known but highly successful guy who had made his fortune selling calendars in shopping centres. The guy was worth $20 million or so and I thought, what better way to fight your way out of the situation than to ring the wealthiest bloke you knew and enlist his counsel.

He said one thing that changed my whole perspective. He said, "Do you think some court judge is even remotely going to care about some tiny little real estate trainer who's having some bullshit fight about nothing? No offence, mate, but the world's got much bigger things to worry about than two blokes having a tiff."

And that's when I realised that I'd been doing it all for me. My original motivations in starting my business had been to survive and an unhealthy obsession to run competitors out of business. I'd chosen the common enemy approach and it wasn't healthy. I switched in that very moment and made the decision to do it for my customers, to help them achieve their potential, to help them reach financial freedom and, above all else, to be a role model.

The next day, I boarded a flight to Queenstown, New Zealand, one of the most amazing cities in the world. As the plane glided well above the snow-capped mountains and we approached descent over the Remarkables, I made the decision to follow my purpose in life. I was going to be the modern-day version of Zig Ziglar and I'd do whatever it took; I'd learn the lessons and get out there and help people to achieve their potential and that would be my driving force.

A whole new wave of energy took over my body and I've never been the same since. The fear-driven, weak individual that had boarded that plane landed with a strong, fearless purpose that would go on to drive all sorts of wonderful and amazing experiences for not only me but for the people around me.

CHAPTER 3: $400 AN HOUR.

I remember being in sixth grade and my Dad picking me up from school, which was rare because that was normally something that mum did. I'd been a victim of some pretty normal schoolyard bullying, so it was my Mum's decision to keep me a little protected.

I wanted to go home, but as I looked up, I saw Dad taking the corner and heading in the opposite direction of home towards work. I was annoyed and said, "Dad can you take me home?" He said "No," and being persistent I continued on my line of enquiry. He refused to answer and finally, after the 10th time, he'd had enough. "Don't you get it? It will take me an hour of my day — an hour I'll never get back to drive you home. I'm worth $400 an hour; now are you going to pay that? You're coming to work and that's it."

Now, for any ten-year-old, that was a hard conversation, to learn that money was more important than your family, but I didn't take it that way at all. I was fascinated. I was getting paid in potato cakes to spend the day with Dad at the open house on Saturdays, worth around 90 cents and here my dad was earning $400 an hour. How many potato cakes could he have with that sort of money? I decided that I wanted to learn as much as I could from this guy and I made the decision to use every waking hour doing my best and never wasting it because time was precious. Let's face it — every hour was worth $400 and that was a lot of potato cakes.

That perspective made me realise that in life you have a choice to make. You either earn by the hour, or you get paid on results and if you're really good, you'll get paid on both. The money is just a scoreboard of how much service you've provided to others, how much you've helped to improve their condition.

I learnt that day that you rise or fall to the level of the people around you and to always negotiate before you sign the deal. I was dealt a crippling blow by my career adviser several years later when she advised that I wouldn't make it to university because I just wasn't smart enough and that I should go to TAFE and see what happened.

There I was faced with the crossroads of disappointing my Dad. I thought there must be a better way. He wanted me to become a property valuer and I didn't want to disappoint, but the marks required were high and mine were low. Learning the value of money at an early age, I decided to make the best of a bad situation.

I went down to the local chamber of commerce as a 16-year-old and got a list of every business in town that had over 50 employees. I had an idea of getting a cadetship. It was something I'd seen the Army recruiters talking about, where they paid for you to go to university, regardless of your marks and gave you a job as soon as you finished. The only problem was I didn't want to join the Army.

So I rang everyone else on that list, asked to speak to the business owner or CEO. After 100 calls I struck gold with two: one a paper manufacturer, the other the local newspaper.

I remember getting in that car, driving across to the newspaper to sell my pitch to the CEO. After being grilled for what felt like hours, I was advised that it was a great idea that they'd pursue and that I'd need to apply. For weeks on end the largest ads they could summon ended up in the paper, all of my mates were applying for the job I had created.

Finally, the day of the interview came and I went in there with the intention of coming out with what I wanted. That CEO did the greatest ever sell on me I'd ever seen to date. He asked me what I wanted, then went and sold me the dream. He advised that the pay would be somewhere between $12 and $25 an hour. Deal accepted.

Weeks later, when I turned up to start, he'd completely forgotten our conversation and I was promptly paid $12 an hour for the next three years. I got my university degree paid for and when I finished, I left after they made the poor decision to offer me a full-time role that paid an extra 38 cents a week.

What I learnt from that is that you have to define what you want and work the formula.

Here's the formula:

- Amount you want to earn + tax + superannuation =
- Divide that by the number of weeks a year you want to work =
- Divide that by the number of hours you want to work a day =

For example: $1m to earn, plus $500,000 for tax and $150,000 for superannuation = $1,650,000 / 44 weeks / 50 hours = $750 per hour.

That's your hourly rate. Now look at that number, minus how much you are currently earning and think that, whatever the difference, this is how much value you need to bring to the table.

You either earn it in cash, or you earn it in learning.

JOSH PHEGAN

CHAPTER 4: BROKEN WINDOWS AND NO VIDEO.

As a business grows, you need to learn from your mistakes. The one I'd made early was having too many of my eggs in one basket. I was speaking at 70 events across Australia and New Zealand and one client had bought 35 of them for the last three years. After a change of management, I got a call late one November and was advised they'd appointed a new state manager. The state manager called to let me know he had to look progressive, so it was time for them to move on.

In just one call, I'd lost 50% of my business overnight. I was beyond stressed. I'd ramped up a team. I'd taken on overhead. I was just starting to get ahead. So I put a plan into action. I called up my videographer and booked him in for the next morning. When he turned up, I had a great idea to film a new video for our clients on why they should use me.

As he set up, I ran into the office to grab a prop for filming and then I ran out. The only challenge is I didn't use the door. I managed to run through a 3m by 3m plate glass window. For some reason, I'd blacked out, just seconds later I found myself surrounded by broken glass. Large chunks of glass crashed to the floor; I was surrounded by it, then the blood started to flow. Everything had gotten too much I couldn't hack the stress. The incident had left me in shock and there I was losing blood like milk down a sink.

The quick-thinking videographer ripped off his shirt, wrapping the wound and drove me down to St Vincent's Hospital in Sydney. I was rushed into the emergency department for emergency surgery on my hand.

How could things go so wrong?

As I watched the nurse sew up my wounds, she asked me how it had happened. Was it drugs, alcohol, a bad relationship, or work stress that had got me to this moment?

I couldn't admit it; I was too proud. Then I told her what had happened, how I'd lost 50% of my business in one day. Her advice that day changed the course of my life.

Here's the nurse's plan:
1. Never sell more than 10% of your diary to any one client.
2. Plan: Don't sell your time for what's just in front of you, sell yourself a year in advance.
3. Enjoy the journey.

And that's exactly what I did. Armed with a new plan, I left the hospital covered in dried blood, a ripped suit jacket and suited pants that had been cut open from the front just above the knee. What a sight. I made the decision that day to always, always plan for a much bigger future and learned an important lesson about always becoming more valuable for your customer so that you're always a logical choice.

CHAPTER 5: MEDIOCRE DREAMS AND BIG DREAMS TAKE THE SAME AMOUNT OF EFFORT.
– LARRY PAGE.

It was time for a new dream. My company had grown quickly from a fledgling start-up without any plans to a wild seven-digit business growing at a rapid 22%, based on that we were doubling our revenue every 3-and-a-bit years.

Things were fast. I'd attracted a great group of people to work with me, but I knew there was more to be had. We landed in America; there, I was with my head of marketing, who'd rapidly helped the business scale to a point where we'd become a real option in the industry.

Just when you think you've got everything sorted, it all changes. We were discussing a vision for the firm and what it takes. We'd both seen Jim Collin's, in his incredible book 'Beyond Entrepreneurship', talk about the vision for a business. You have to have a purpose (the reason why you do what you do for the customer), a mission (critical growth marks on your journey to success in real, measurable numbers) and values (the rules of the game).

Purpose was easy: We worked hard to inspire estate agents to achieve their potential and their financial freedom. Values were easy for us too, we'll explore these more in the book but here's a quick summary:

1. We work free of time and space. I'd always been on the road; our whole company was virtual from day one and we'd never worked in an office.

2. We innovate and constantly improve. Incremental innovation leads to breakthroughs and that wins markets.

3. We perform at our best in everything we do. When you do your best, whether you win or lose, you always win because the lessons are the greatest teachers.

4. We renew our energy. Energy matters and it's your job to renew it. People love fresh; they hate tired and drawn.

5. We believe in people and their dreams.

Then it hit me that if we believed in people and their dreams, then it was time to dream a new dream. My head of marketing turned to me at that point and said one thing that changed the course of our entire business. "I didn't realise that when I joined this company that I was also given a life sentence." Those words pierced every chamber of my heart. "What do you mean?" I muttered out. "I didn't realise that you just want me to be your head of marketing forever. Believe it or not, I actually have dreams, aspirations and ambitions well above just working in this little company you know."

Done. It was the turning point into a whole new way of thinking. If it was to be, it was up to me. The bigger the dream, the more important the team. What I worked out is that I hadn't set the vision, I didn't drive the purpose, nor did I run to the rules of the business — the values. My number one job as the leader was to set the vision, to inspire others through action.

Fast forward just two short years later and you'd find me on a plane flying back from Christchurch in New Zealand. I don't know what it was about New Zealand, but I think a three-hour flight was just enough to get you thinking about what's really going on. I was speaking at over 168 events a year in two different countries and we were sold out 9 months in advance. Things were brisk. But there was something bugging me. How were we going to achieve the growth? I had big dreams, but I needed to work out the way to do it.

That's when it hit me.

CHAPTER 6: BUSINESS IS THE ULTIMATE SPORT. – MARK CUBAN

There it was. I drew two giant rectangles. I labelled one potential, the other capacity and put a measure on them from 0 to 100%.

Now it was time for two important definitions:
- Potential: What you are capable of as a human being.
- Capacity: Your ability to do more.

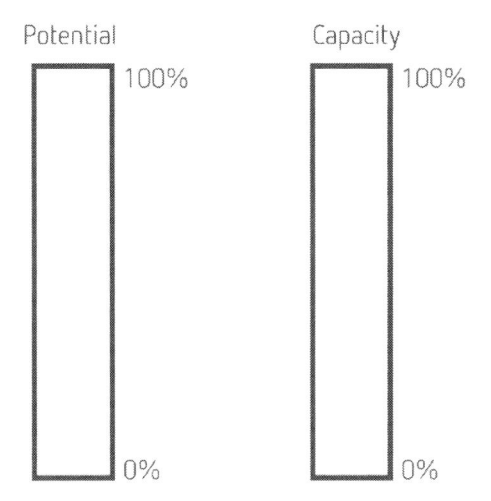

```
  Potential              Capacity
   ┌─────┐                ┌─────┐
   │100% │                │100% │
   │     │                │     │
   │     │                │     │
   │     │                │     │
   │     │                │     │
   │ 0%  │                │ 0%  │
   └─────┘                └─────┘
```

I started colouring. I'd read a fascinating book by Atul Gawande called

Being Mortal and in that he said:

"We are young to the degree that our ambitions are greater than our memories."

So over the past few months I'd be grinding away at my ambition: What did I want to become? What was I capable of?

Two important questions emerged:
- What does success look like to you?
- And how will you know when you've achieved it?

I truly thought that my potential was only 13%, as I had a much bigger game to play. Then I coloured in my capacity. My calendar was full, I was flat stick. I coloured it in to 99%.

I had nothing left. How was I supposed to fulfil my potential without the capacity? What follows is my no-holds-barred approach on achieving more potential by opening up my capacity.

What you soon work out is that, as you build more capacity, you find a brand new world out there. You open up to your potential.

"May the space between your dreams and your reality inspire you." —Unknown.

CHAPTER 7: IF YOU DON'T MAKE THE DECISION TO F!*KING BACK YOURSELF IN, WHO WILL? – DAVID BROWN

When I first went to start my business, I'd had a call from an earlier mentor. He'd pushed me to develop a vision of what I'd wanted. The truth was, I wanted a job where the future was so exciting that I never had to sleep in the same bed for more than two nights in a row. I wanted to see the world.

He was talking to me one night while I was sitting on the fence about whether to start or not and in a heated exchange over the phone, he told me straight out, "You need to f*&king back yourself in; no one else is going to."

CHAPTER 8: YOUR BIGGEST CHALLENGE IS THAT YOU'LL NEVER BE SUCCESSFUL BECAUSE YOU'VE JUST GOT YOUR TOE IN THE WATER; IF YOU DIVE IN YOU MIGHT JUST HAVE A FIGHTING CHANCE. — CHRIS JONES

Things changed rapidly once I drew that diagram. I realised that I had to change something. I had two choices: either rapidly decrease my ambition and lower my expectations around my potential, or rapidly find a way to build new capacity. I worked out that I was lonely in business; there was no one to really share the wins or the loses with and I was doing all the heavy lifting.

In just a few seconds it came to me: There is a formula for success, I had it right there in my hand. Here's the formula that will change your life.

To increase capacity = Fitness + Systems + People

Let's define them.

Fitness = The speed of your recovery. If you run up a hill, your heart rate increases. When you get to the top of the hill and stop, you breathe in heavy. The quicker that your heart rate gets back to it's resting heart rate, that's known as your fitness. Fitness wasn't just physical; it was mental and emotional. Hell, there was business fitness, life fitness, crisis fitness and about a million others depending on where they come from.

Systems = A way of doing things, that if done the same way each time, produces the same desired result with little variation. Systems would become a massive part of my business and rapidly change everything.

People = Once you've got the systems, you're ready for the people to join your business and take everything over, so you can concentrate on what truly makes you great.

What I'd learned is that people had it flipped the wrong way in business. They hired people with no plan, they had no systems and when it all fell to pieces, they had to rapidly get fit again. That wasn't for me.

CHAPTER 9: WHAT DRIVES YOU?

There are three motivations that drive human effort:

1. Family and friends. What we do for them, the experiences we get to share, their advice and guidance and just being there for them — that drives purpose for many people. Ask a new mum or a doting father and they'll respond.
2. Who are you becoming? If you come from a humble beginning, you should open like a flower to the sun to realise that there is a world out there for you to explore and add value to and that you can achieve something much bigger than the dreams you were instilled with.
3. Who or what are you building? A cause like curing cancer, providing better food in school canteens, or building an investment portfolio, a record company, or an electric car company. Whatever it is, it drives you like there's no tomorrow.

Often, for many, they are moving away from pain and they don't want anyone else to experience the pain they've gone through. Mine was a drive to build something great, to help people achieve their potential and reach financial freedom. I just had this desire as a young kid to help, to find a way to do more with less. Coming from the country, it forces you to be creative.

The most powerful people are those who have all three motivations. It provides a deep purpose that's never ending. Our purpose can also change over time, as shifting priorities move the goal posts on what's possible.

CHAPTER 10: LIVE A LIFE YOU'D RE-LIVE. GOALS MATTER.

I'd heard it all before. If one more person wanted to tell me to get some goals, I was gonna tell them where to go. The problem with goals is that they irritate you if you don't have them, you're directionless and you find yourself way off course when you define your purpose.

The problem with goals is that they tend to be wants and wants change over time. When I was a little kid, I got a Matchbox car for good behaviour, a Ferrari. I really liked it and decided I wanted one when I grew up. The challenge doesn't exactly get me out of bed in the morning to go and get one, because your wants change as you get older.

An unsatisfied need is a motivator of behaviour. The opposite of this is that a satisfied need is not a motivator of behaviour. So, here's a better question: what are your unsatisfied needs? Find those and you'll dive deeply into biting off more than you can chew.

CHAPTER 11: THE QUESTIONS YOU ASK AND THE ANSWERS YOU GIVE.

The questions that you've asked and the answers that you've given have gotten you here, so what are the questions you need to ask or the answers you need to change to get you to where you want to go?

I'm playing with you. You need to hook onto something strong in the future, then winch your way there. We call it a personal Everest. Your personal Everest is made up of all the unidentified, unmet and unsatisfied needs you have. It starts with your purpose – what you're here to do. Plenty of us struggle to find that, then we discover that life is about the experiences you have and the people you get to share them with. If you put yourself in enough situations, you'll figure it out, just as I did.

James C Collins, better known as Jim Collins, wrote about it in his fascinating book *Beyond Entrepreneurship*. He said that a business needs a vision and that vision is made up of its purpose, mission and values.

Purpose is something that is never ending. Even when you pass from this earth, that purpose will be ongoing, taken up by someone else to further the cause.

One of my favourites is Johnson and Johnson. They make baby products, talcum powder and Band Aids. What could their purpose be? It's not about making profits; it's actually to alleviate pain. They look for painful situations then find ways to fix them.

Microsoft's vision is to put a computer on every desk in the world. Up until 2012, they didn't even make computers. They worked out that they needed to produce the software that made the computers more useful more often.

Nike's vision is to empower every athlete, so when you put on your running shorts and running top, you feel like you're Usain Bolt.

When you discover your purpose, you'll know it, but don't worry about it. Just throw yourself into more experiences, more often.

The second part to your personal Everest is discovering your personal mission. A mission is a specific, measurable goal, that can easily be defined, for example, write $1m in fees, sell 100 houses, manage 1000 properties. With your mission, set it out 5 years ahead, make it audacious and get clear on your KPI's, the key numbers you need to monitor. Now your job is to find a way to achieve them. When you set forth on a bigger goal, new worlds, ways of thinking and relationships open up to you as you ask will this or won't this get me to where I want to go?

The secret, as one of my best friends, April Forbes, puts it, is "Don't change the plan, let the plan change you."

The final part in you vision is your values, or the rules by which you play the game. Verne Harnish says it best: "A business is a lot like a family; it needs a set of rules that you live by," to keep behaviour in alignment. We'll discover the importance of values later in this book.

CHAPTER 12: WE ARE YOUNG TO THE DEGREE THAT OUR AMBITION IS GREATER THAN OUR MEMORIES. — ATUL GAWANDE.

Wow, what a quote. Since I read that in Atul Gawande's incredible book, *Being Mortal,* I have never been the same. The reason why we fumble, why life changes for us, why some people seem old and others have a youthful energy about them despite their age, comes down to one thing: Purpose. You have to have something in front of you that you want to achieve, at all times, period, or else you'll age. That's the whole problem with the notion of retirement, that it's OK to have some deferred sense of living at the end. I'd rather live every day, so to stay young I drive my ambition, grinding away at it everyday. The more that you work on what you want and not just the tangible stuff, the more purpose you have and the bigger the energy required to do it. What you thought was busy five years ago, isn't busy by today's measuring stick. The world has sped up, but so have you if you've been grinding away at your ambition and using the right systems to continually develop self.

Here is the process you go through:

Incremental growth
Day by day, look for new ways to do things. Just by being around enough, you see people doing things with ease that you've struggled with. We use a methodology taught to us by Peter Knight, from the Property Academy in the UK, called WWW.EBI. It stands for: What worked well? And even better if. . . ? Answering those two questions about your performance after every

event, every day, every time you do something that you want to do better, forces improvement over time. You're constantly tweaking for continuous improvement.

Breakthroughs

When you face a significant barrier, hopefully, it forces you to gather new energy, new insights and new perspectives to find your way. A breakthrough happens when you didn't think you'd be able to do what you do, but you gain highly valuable insight or come up with a way to do what you wanted to do. The feeling, the rush of blood to the head at that very moment when the breakthrough happens, is truly something else. You'll know it when it happens.

Game changers

Sometimes you're forced into a new way of doing things. New technologies, changes in society and the environment force a complete rewrite of the old way of doing things. Mobile phones have enabled so much change in so many aspects of our lives. We've sped them up to the point that most of us spend hours trying to slow them down, not realising that the pace of life right now is the slowest it will be for the rest of our lives.

CHAPTER 13: THE TRUTH.

You will never be ready and you can't predict too much of the future, but what you can do is play with a solid set of rules to enable a much bigger future.

You do that by working out that no-one's got it figured out. A big part of success is about being in the right place at the right time.

I wanted to systemise success because I found it all too random. Why is it that some people come to a training room, write a tonne of notes, then go away and become superstars, while others turn up to the same session, judge it, come with their bias and claim it was a waste of their time?

Well, it comes down to this: some people have hooked on to a future where they know that learning is the only way. The quicker you adapt, the more you do; that's where success comes from.

As you grow and scale and more importantly, as you reach your potential, you'll find all sorts of ways to increase your capacity. The role is to reduce the load so that the stress doesn't get too much over the long term. Short-term is way fine, that's called growth. Long-term is dangerous and shows a complete lack of bigger future thinking.

You've created the world that you live in and you have the power to change it.

CHAPTER 14: FITNESS ISN'T JUST PHYSICAL.

Here are all the areas of fitness:

- Business Fitness
- Prospecting Fitness
- Listing Presentation Fitness
- Negotiation Fitness
- Holiday Fitness
- Relationship Fitness
- Time Management Fitness
- Physical Fitness
- Emotional Fitness
- Buyer Work Fitness
- Delegation Fitness
- Qualification Fitness
- Vendor Work Fitness
- Days On Market Fitness
- Auction Fitness
- Fee Fitness
- Selling Vendor Paid Marketing Fitness
- Clarity Of The Future Fitness
- Crisis Fitness
- Measurement Fitness
- Ambition Fitness

- Goals Fitness
- Lifestyle Fitness
- Spiritual Fitness

Every one of them needs work and the longer you leave them the harder it is to get them to their optimum state. You need great people around you, people you can hook on to that can become mentors in each area, to hold you to high account and help you achieve your potential in each. It's OK to feel overwhelmed initially, but soon you'll learn that you can have it all if you put in the work, find a way and take guidance from others.

CHAPTER 15: FITNESS OVER SICKNESS. IRONTRIBE.

Being a systems guy, I went into a crazy period of working out all the bio hacks to improve my fitness. I started with physical fitness and here's what I learned.

If you don't have time for fitness, then how will you ever make time for sickness? Disease, if broken, becomes dis-ease, that is, no comfort. That's not the way I wanted to live. I'd been to see one of the great oracles in the world, Sue McCarthy, at the Kangaroo Island Health Retreat and over our years together, I'd come to build some simple rules. Fitness isn't just physical, but it's a great place to start, because you can't have discipline in one area of your life and not have it in others.

The areas I've focused on for physical fitness are:

Diet
There are plenty of people who don't want to be on a diet, but what you eat is your diet. So whether you like it or not we're all on a diet.

The goal is three meals a day, so that's 21 meals a week. Out of those 21 meals, 16 of those meals must be to your dietary plan. The dietary plan that works is to divide your plate into:
- 10% fatty acids like nuts, seeds and avocado that lubricate the brain
- 20% lean protein; this is anything from an animal, like yoghurt, meats and the bean family
- 70% simple carbs; these are vegetables. My basic rule here is that if you have to cook it, it's complex

You can lay another rule over the top of that, that 50% of your plate must be raw/uncooked

No meal can be consumed in under 20 minutes, so if you have to, divide your plate into four quarters and you've got 5 minutes for each

The water rule

This one rule will give you absolute focus. I aim for two litres a day and in my peak, three. Room temperature water is best, as it's absorbed by the body. No drinking for 20 minutes prior, during the course of, or for one hour after eating. I like to get a litre in before breakfast, a litre during the day and a litre just before going to bed. I guarantee that you'll never have any issues getting out of bed in the morning.

Every time you reach for something that you shouldn't be having, have a litre of water first and tell me if you still want it. It stops the manic over-eating and keeps you fighting fit.

Think that if a human touched it, it's probably not good for you. If it comes unpackaged, it's probably good.

To drive success, I schedule when I eat because health is my number one priority. It's the only thing you can't buy. As my schedule gets more hectic, it's even more important to follow a routine. I aim to eat breakfast at 6.30am, lunch at 12pm and dinner at 6pm. Ideally, it's four to six hours between each meal. I place those as appointments in my diary and hold on to them like there's no tomorrow. What and how you eat determine what happens in your life. If you're manic and unscheduled, so will your life be.

Exercise

Tony Schwartz wrote a fascinating book called *The Power Of Full Engagement* and in that book, he dialled in on human performance. Exercise is the body's natural stress release valve. From age 30 until you die, you lose half a kilo of lean body muscle that turns into fat without active intervention. That's why you need to do weights, ideally every day, to maintain and build your muscle mass. If you keep your muscles maintained and growing, you can carry more in life and keep yourself upright as you get older.

I love to run; it's been a saviour and it lets me see the world. I was never a runner until my late 20's. A good friend challenged me to run 5 km with her one day and I've been chasing her every since. It's free, easy to do and it gives you fresh air.

What I've found is that the way I exercise is the way I run my business. I set a simple goal: 5 km's per day Monday through Friday (with one of those days as a day of rest if I need it), a 10 km run by the ocean every Sunday, (ideally) 3-4 weight sessions every week with a personal trainer and a TRX Group session every Saturday to add the social element to my training. There's nothing quite like having someone push you to be your best.

Every year I review the workout, the plan and the results and adjust where needed. Stretching and mobility become critical, the way you move at 30 has a massive bearing on how you'll move at 50, 70 and 100.

How old will you be when you die?

I'll never forget, one evening at the health retreat when Sue was talking to me about life; she looked me dead in the eye and said, "How old will you be when you die?" The question hit me hard. I'd never given any thought to it. She asked me to work that out by tomorrow or else we couldn't work together anymore.

I had a restless nights' sleep that night trying to work out when I was going to die. The next morning, I sprung up for our 21 km soft sand beach walk and her first word of the day was "...and?" "100 plus, Sue. That'll do."

"Great," she said, "and is the way you're living today consistent with the way you want to be living at a 100? Are you doing everything to preserve, maintain and grow the mind, body and spirit?" She had a point. So I found ROMWOD, a daily stretching and flexibility workout that got me moving, improved my running times and helped me to touch my toes.

Sleep

There's a tonne of research on sleep, so I'll be brief. The most important thing for me is a regular bedtime. I'm for a sleep time of 10pm every night and I rise every day at 4.10am. I was never an early riser, but I want to take as many shots in life as possible. I sleep in as a reward on Sundays, until 5.10 am. By drinking a litre of room temperature water before I go to bed, I have no problem rising in the morning. I've trained my body to retain the water whilst I sleep, so I'm super fast to get out of bed every morning.

To improve my sleep, I have a weekly massage for an hour, to get the blood moving around the body and a 30-minute sauna every week, to remove any water retention. Your body holds more water in areas it shouldn't when you get stressed, so this is an awesome driver for success and will keep you at your best.

CHAPTER 16: MENTAL ENERGY MATTERS.

In the middle of a crisis, you need coping mechanisms, as teaching yourself how to deal with tough situations and training yourself for routine will set you free.

I follow a simple, rule-based circadian and ultridium rhythms, basically, the reasons why your body wants to stay awake during the day and go to sleep at night time. Your body runs in 90-minute cycles, hence why if you hit the snooze button on the alarm clock and go back to sleep, that you feel more tired and sluggish than if you had of just got up, as now you're into your next 90-minute cycle.

I didn't always have the routine, but I've trained myself to be a gun in short periods of time. In the early days I'd set a 45 minute timer and during that 45 minutes all I'd do is work. There are no distractions: no Facebook, no Instagram, no mobile, no TV—nothing. Just work for that 45 minutes. I use those 45-minute sessions for clearing email, to calling out to potential clients.

I learnt early that the first 45 minutes of every day should be spent in marketing, so every business day I send a daily email at 4:15am. It's based on the issues of the day and how you can achieve your potential. It's how I built my business in the early days, committing to doing just that one thing. Over time I've added a weekly coaching video, a weekly podcast and a monthly growth, leadership and management video. But there's one thing that will also make your business great and that's to call your customers for a minimum of 45 minutes a day.

I've conducted over 1,000 45-minute call sessions for clients around the world and here are the results:

During a 45-minute call session:
You'll call on average 16 – 24.
Connect to 8 – 12.
Book appointments with 1 – 3.

Imagine that 50% of all the calls you make end up in a voicemail, so get good at leaving voicemails. I just leave my name and mobile number, never the reason for my call. You should see the call-backs.

Also, 50% of calls end up in a connection and one in every three ends up in an appointment.

I've trained my mental energy by working to a routine. Here's the routine that's really worked.

- 4.10 am - Wake
- 4.15 am - Daily email goes out
- 4.20 am - Run time
- 4.30 am - PT
- 5.00 am - Run home.
- 5.30 am - Clear my emails and get prepared for the day and week ahead.
- 6.15 am - Shower and pack.
- 6.30 am - Breakfast
- 6.50 am - First phone call in the car on the way to a client.
- 7.00 am - Phone my head of sales to check in for the day and to start the day right.
- 7.30 am - Arrive at my client's for work.
- 8.00 am - Showtime, the show begins.
- 9.40 am - Morning tea.
- 12.00 pm - Lunch for 30 minutes.
- 12.30 pm - Consulting with the client.
- 3.00 pm - Finish time.
- 3.00 pm - 4.00 pm - Check in with my team.
- 4.00 pm - 6.00 pm - Coaching calls in the car or on a walk.
- 6.00 pm - Dinner
- 6.30 pm - Flight to my next destination, or clear emails and prepare until 7.30 pm.
- 7.30 pm - 10.00 pm - Check in with family and friends.

I do that on repeat for 5 days of a week and keep a similar schedule on Saturdays. Sundays I like to keep as a free day for renewal and apart from my morning run just see what happens.

Now you might think that the above is crazy talk and so did I, until I lived it and now I love it. I work like that for 44 weeks of the year and have 8 weeks of annual leave a year.

When I holiday, I'm probably one of the only people I know that comes back fitter from a holiday then when I left, because I have even more time to focus on my health. Your health never goes on holiday; remember that, so work with it.

CHAPTER 17: WHEN ANXIETY, INSECURITY AND LACK OF CONFIDENCE TAKE YOU OUT.

Every year, it happened at the same time. Just a few hours before heading out to celebrate New Year's Eve, I'd get reflective; I'd look inward and become worried that another year had gone by while I'd done nothing. This overwhelming anxiety and insecurity would overtake me and I just couldn't handle it anymore.

Then, I saw this quote:

The reason that we struggle with insecurity is that we're comparing our behind-the-scenes with everyone else's highlight reel. – Unknown.

How true. With the rise and growth of social media, we see more people with perfect lives, more perfect than ours. In fact, we're all human and we all put our jeans on one leg at a time. Remember that humility matters. Work hard, stay humble.

CHAPTER 18: HAVE AN INNER SCORECARD FOR SUCCESS AND DON'T CARE WHAT ANYONE ELSE EVER SAYS. – WARREN BUFFETT.

Then, I realised that everything in life is either a system or a person and if you're not getting what you want, you need to develop with one of those if you want significant progress. So, here's the system.

1. **Write out your goals and put them in your phone.**
   Here are the categories I use:
   - Physical - Ideal weight: what you want your body to do, feel and be
   - Health - Overall health including workouts, diet, sleep
   - Professional - Career and business aspirations
   - Mental - Developing the way you think, by exposing yourself more often to new experiences
   - Family - Connectedness and growth
   - Key relationships - Which ones I want to work on and grow
   - Travel - Where you want to go in the world to open you up to new experiences
   - Adventure - The things that put a grin on your face, when you feel your heart beating through your chest, the photo moments
   - Creativity - Exploring your potential and what your capable of, creating things anew

- Legacy - What you'll be remembered for
- Character - The way you carry yourself
- Spiritual - Your connectedness to the world and those around you
- Financial - Your active (money you earn by doing the work) and passive incomes (money you earned without being involved, rent from property, dividends from shares in a business and interest form money in the bank)

Dan Sullivan has a great thought on this in his podcast, *the 10 X multipliers*. Imagine that you want to take the long-term perspective. Write down your current age today and add 25.

That's how old you'll be in 25 years. What do you want in each of those areas?

It's hard, isn't it? That is, until you take the approach from the film the Matrix — the red pill or the blue pill. It's about making decisions one at a time and developing a bigger vision. There are four quarters in a year, so multiply that by 25 years and that's 100 quarters. Therefore, one quarter is equal to one per cent of the goal.

Every year, I seek out mentorship in every category of my goals. I want someone whom I admire in each of those areas for what they bring to the game. I seek them out and spend time with them. They challenge me to achieve my potential, to play a much bigger game.

No one came here to play it small.

2. Then write down your achievements as they happen.

Every Sunday when I run Bondi to Coogee Beach, I stop at the 5km mark and pull out my phone. In my notes section, I have my achievements list. There, I write down every great thing that happened for me that week. Usually, I'll have three to five items and it doesn't seem like much, but it gives you perspective. When I get to the end of the year, I've got somewhere between 150 and 250 achievements for the year.

Whenever I'm not feeling it, I just read over my achievements list and realise how far I've come. It's amazing because that achievements list usually forms the base plate for next years' goals. There's a lot of reoccurring goals like health, financial success, etc. and all you need to do is tweak and increase them and this fuels your capacity, the more you achieve, the more ambitious you become.

This is the number one chief confidence builder that will literally change your life and the life of those around you. I've had clients do it with their kids and completely change their relationships, not to mention the confidence it builds in others to bite off even more audacious goals.

It's free, costs you nothing, but puts you on an almighty path to achievement and success.

3. **Lessons learned list**

I never thought I'd need this, but I do and it's awesome. Every time something goes wrong in my life, I write it down on my lessons learned list in my phone. It's an awesome list of every area where you don't have a system or a person, or either of those just isn't working. What first starts out as a negative becomes an awesome list of opportunities for further improvement. Whenever a staff member, a family member, or in fact anyone in my life find themselves in a position of vulnerability, we celebrate it by writing it down on their lessons learned list and quickly move on to creating a much bigger future.

Task lists matter. As more things come flying at you, how are you going to remember what's been done and what's still on your plate?

I use a really simple daybook where I write down all the things that need to be done as they come at me. My goal is to do that list. You can use great online systems, but there's nothing quite like the feeling of crossing something off.

Emotional energy matters.

CHAPTER 19: IT'S NOT THE WORDS YOU USE, IT'S HOW YOU MAKE PEOPLE FEEL THAT MATTERS.

It's an amazing to learn. Every time I found myself being negative, depressed or wanting to get out of the game, I realised I was in my head thinking about poor me rather than being out of my head and thinking about how I could help others. Then, I realised that my contribution to others is what matters. I realised that we all have an awesome responsibility to be the chief confidence-builder in others, which in turn will build our confidence.

NEXT - it's the most important word you'll ever learn. When something happens to you that changes your mood for the worse, realise that these emotions now own you. When you pour out negativity, it affects you far more than it does the other person. So, instead, I choose to say, "Next!" and move on. Emotional recovery matters and there are two major sources of it.

1. Music is an emotion changer. I'm convinced that if you play the same piece of music over and over, it's a trigger for living out experiences or bringing about a certain mood. Before every training session, I play the same music to remind me to perform at my best—after all, any day could be your last. I've got musical trigger tracks that trigger emotions from really important memories or states and help me to perform at my best. When I reach a big moment, I play the same piece of music over and over so that I can use that as a trigger for the emotional, sensory recall of what happened at that moment.

2. Relationships are the key to renewal. Ever spent 15 minutes with someone and just felt like that sucked the living daylight out of you? Ever

spent 15 minutes with someone and got so wrapped in the moment because of that person's amazing energy? Well, that's exactly what great relationships will do — they help you to renew. I'm a big believer in only having relationships where 1) I can help; 2) there's a mutual benefit, in that I give and they take, or they give and I take, but it works both ways; and 3) we both have a bigger future working together.

I've cut some relationships that were hard to cut, but it was really important for my personal growth.

CHAPTER 20: VALUES MATTER.

Values are the rules of how you play the game. – Verne Harnish.

I could never understand why some people just rubbed me up the wrong way. Then I realised I just don't like the way they played the game.

I went in search of a better way to run my business and I keep running into this conversation about values. So what were the rules that allowed us to play the game the way it should be played?

First, I wrote down the key words that are important to me.

High performance – the name of our podcast and everything I'm about: doing everything you can with all you've got
Energy – because the energy you put out there is the energy you get back
Mutuality – fairness and equality for all, because we're all human, just trying to do our best through this thing called life
Respect – respecting other people and their opinions
Financial freedom – because we should never let our financial situation limit who we can become

I had some words and now I had some rules. But there was a challenge; even though I knew them and I'd put them into the letters of offer for my team, we weren't really living them. I reapplied that the soldiers only ever do what the generals do. So, the number one person who had to live out the values was me.

The challenge with individual words is that they can be

misinterpreted easily. My version of high performance might be very different from your version of high performance. I needed a better system. I took the words and created something different, ideally five short sentences, of up to five or so words, each one communicating the spirit behind those values.

In our company today, I'm super proud to say that everyone knows our values. We talk about them every time we meet and they're on our one-page plan and in our weekly check-ins. We worked and worked and worked to get our rules in place and now they serve us very well to ensure we have the right behaviours.

CHAPTER 21: THE FIVE VALUES OF THE JOSH PHEGAN COMPANY.

1.   We work free of time and space.

No matter where we are or what we're doing, we have the capability to work. We don't have to be in an office to make it happen. In fact, we've never worked as a team in an office and although we have one in Sydney, I've only sat at my desk there for an hour in the last five years. It's really become a loading dock where things get delivered. We work from our homes, from airport lounges, or from coffee shops because we believe in hiring freak talent that can work from anywhere they are.

2.   We innovate and constantly improve.

The only thing that keeps me involved in this business is growth: of our clients, our people and me. It's exciting to work out how to bring the formula to achieve more every year and sometimes with less. Innovation is at the heart of all great businesses as it involves incremental improvements that help you to deliver more. We work with a fascinating speaker named Peter Knight in the UK and he uses the acronym www.ebi, which stands for "What worked well?" "And even better if?" Every time we finish off something big, we pull out the www.ebi model and look to where we can do better.

3.   We renew our energy.

If you're going to play at your best, you have to bring your best energy to the table. When you're sick, tired and burned out, you're no good to anyone, including your family. No one wants you when you're like that, so it's your number-one priority to keep your energy at its best. Diet, exercise and sleep matter. So we're big in our company to make sure that we cater to our clients like that. This is why our team exercises at our team events and we get appropriate time off the grid.

4. We perform at our best in everything that we do.

This one is critical. Work to the standard and perform at your best. No half-baked work, only the best you can do. We're all about improvement and when a staff member joins our company, we give them the 10 books they need to read in their first year, so they can become more valuable to us. The more valuable they become, the more we can pay them. Think about it this way: now that you've left school, how do you learn? In our team every month, we ask what our people are reading and we see a real difference in who our people become. It wasn't always like this; we faced plenty of resistance. But what I worked out is that I love people who are great learners. And great learners will do what it takes. They'll invest in their own personal and professional development. My dad would give agents in his office two books, *The Art of Selling* and *The Art of Listing* by the great Tom Hopkins. In those books, he'd write in pencil on a certain page that when you got to that page, you should come and see him for a free lunch. In over 30 years, I was the first and only salesperson who went to see him to collect the lunch. All the time, I meet people who tell me they don't like reading and I respond with, "Well, that's a choice. I also choose not to like people who don't read." You should see their reactions. I've helped turned non-readers to high-use Kindle users.

5. We believe in people and their dreams.

This one really got to my heart, realising that we help to build people up, that we are the chief confidence-builders in people's lives. Our role is to help people discover their dreams, to drive their ambitions, to help them achieve them. For years, we've run our annual Changed Agents Awards, where we ask Real Estate Agents from across Australia to submit an application on what they've learned from us in training and how they've put that into their business lives and seen massive results. It's incredibly rewarding when you see just how much people have turned their lives around. Often, we need permission to dream a new dream. Grind away every day at the person you're becoming and, as Dan Sullivan says, "Make sure you have a bigger future than your past."

Now, here's a better question: now that you've got the values, what systems do you use to ensure that your people live them out?

All of my staff have a goals, achievements and lessons-learned list on their phones, so it's super easy to reconnect them with what matters and build their self-confidence.

We also use tools like 15Five, which is an online survey tool that checks on the pulse of the company and gets our team to give an example of another staff member who's lived out one of our values for the week. As a business owner, it gives your staff 15 minutes to write out their feedback on how they're doing against some predefined questions; then it gives you as their manager five minutes to respond once you log in.

Values are everything in business; they are the gold standard to which you hold your people. It reminds me of the old saying: What happens if I train my people and they go? What happens if you don't train your people and they stay? I'm proud to say that every person who's ever worked with us has never left the same person that came; they've always improved and grown brand new skills that have allowed them to live even bigger futures.

CHAPTER 22: BUSINESS FITNESS MATTERS.

What's the job you do for your customers?
Why do they find that to be valuable?

These are two great questions and if you can answer them precisely, you know your business. What I love about small business is the ability to pivot quickly, to test often and go with it.

I believe that business fitness comes down to understanding these factors:
1. How you acquire your leads.
2. How you nurture your clients.
3. How you increase the lifetime spending of your customers.

How do you acquire your leads?
The best question here is "Where do your customers hang out before they need you?" Once you answer that, hang out there. Ultimately, what this leads to is a real understanding of your company's purpose. And purpose is everything. It's bigger than any one person. It's the thing you'll never finish and never complete.

Here're are some of my favourites:
To alleviate pain – Johnson and Johnson.
To empower every athlete – Nike.
A computer on every desk in the world – Microsoft.

Our purpose is simple, to inspire estate agents to achieve their potential and accomplish financial freedom.

So what do we need to do that?

The formula is simple. Write out a list of everyone you know, get close to them, find out what their fears/challenges are and provide the very best solutions. Every day, write to your clients through our daily email, send out our weekly coaching video, our weekly podcast with the number one agent in the country, Alexander Phillips and our monthly growth leadership and management tip. Then, make a minimum of 50 connected phone calls a day. It seems simple in retrospect, but it has built massive demand and continues to drive deeper relationships day by day.

How do you nurture your leads?

Once you've met your clients, it's up to you to drive the value. You need to be everywhere your customer is, be it on social media, in the letterbox, face to face, or over the phone. It's that simple. I learnt something from Virgin Australia: on the first day of every month, they'd have their new magazine on the back seat of every seat, on every plane in the country. That's amazing efficiency. I thought I should do the same. I reasoned that if you send out a piece of marketing once a quarter, then you only give your clients 4 times a year to put up their hands and say they need help. If I did it 12 times, that's 12 times a year they can scream out for help. We work on over 365 connections with each of our clients every year, so there's plenty of opportunity.

The lifetime spending of your customer matters.

What we know is that on average, Australians will buy up to five houses in their lifetimes. So if every transaction is worth a $10,000 fee, that means every client is worth $50,000 in their lifetime. But they are worth far more than that; if they refer me to just one client, who also has five transactions to do, it means every client is now worth over $300,000 in fees, based on their own spending and the spending they refer. Why do people refer you? People refer you because you are really good at what you do, not because you gave them a bottle of champagne. Treat your referrer as though they are the customer, keep them in the loop at all times and watch what happens. You want the referrer to see the person in the street they referred and have a conversation and you want to receive amazing feedback on what you were like to work with and how appreciative they are for being in touch with you.

That's what matters. We live in the experience economy.

Business fitness is therefore about standards. Here's my favourite example on standards:

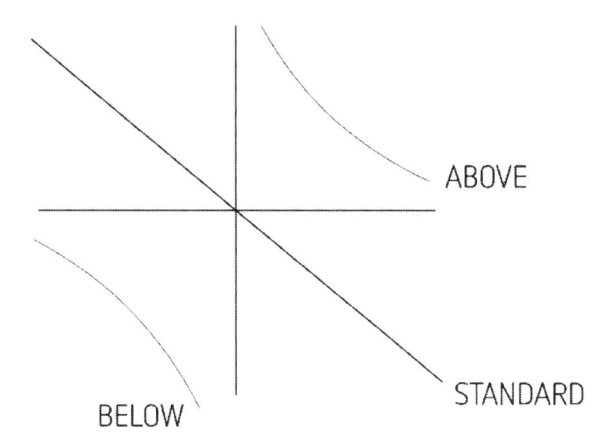

[Diagram showing axes with curves labeled ABOVE, STANDARD, and BELOW]

Let's say we go to the coffee shop and order a coffee. When the coffee comes out, the milk is good, the coffee is the right temperature, there's a beautiful taste and aroma and it's delivered to standard.

The next time we go to the coffee shop and order, the coffee comes out again, but this time with a tiny teddy on the teaspoon. This is now above our expectations. As we keep going to the coffee shop, the tiny teddy keeps on coming out and what was above our expectations soon becomes the norm.

One day, we go to the coffee shop and order the coffee, but there's no tiny teddy. It's now below our expectations. Expectations being met are what keep customers coming back.

I'm not interested in you giving me 110% or delivering 6-star service, especially if you don't even know what it is or how to deliver it. It's even worse if you claim to give it but don't charge for it. What I want is the standard to be delivered every time. I just want consistency.

Two things to be careful of:

Margin.
Business is all about the margins. Most estate agents charge what they think their competitors charge. If you operated this way and were a retailer, you'd be broke in seconds. A retailer has a simple pricing formula -- the cost of goods plus an operating margin plus a profit margin plus a negotiation margin to arrive at the final recommended retail price. So to

get your pricing right, find out how much it costs you to deliver your service, add the appropriate margins and never charge less than that. I'd rather have a profitable market share than just market share.

Scale.

Whilst it sounds great to deliver amazing service, can you do it if you have 10 times more customers? What about 100 times more customers? Always build your service for far more customers than you think you'll ever have and watch it grow as you delight your customers with your consistent service.

CHAPTER 23: BUSINESS RULES FOR EXPANSION WILL SET YOU FREE.

If you want to take new markets by storm, it's much easier and profitable to find someone else who already has the customers you want to reach. We got lucky in the early days. I met Damien Cooley in Sydney and as Sydney's leading auctioneer, he already had the client base I wanted.

I'm eternally grateful and loyal, as loyalty matters. Over the following few years, he'd go on to refer me; I've always done the right thing and it's opened markets for me. We sell out now in the UK thanks to Peter Knight at the Property Academy and the reason for that is the same.

If I'm growing a real estate business, I much prefer to buy out an existing competitor. Why?

1. They already have some market share.
2. They already have an existing lease/location.
3. They already have an existing customer base.
4. I love buying assets that are underperforming and then helping them to perform.

Here are the five basic rules that see exceptional growth amongst our clients if you follow these when you are expanding:

1. You must have a lead agent as a co-director. Lead agents set the pace and the market share and they bring the customer base with them. Ideally, they are already writing $1 million in fees.

2. Buy an existing business, ideally with a property management portfolio of at least 300 managements. This gives you consistent cash flow and it allows at least two property managers; so, one can go on holiday and the business still runs. You get an operating lease and, hopefully, infrastructure that works. It might not be brand-new, but you'll pay nothing for it. You can always rebrand.
3. A logical extension from your existing operations. Far enough away to open new markets, close enough to be culturally in alignment.
4. Ability to recruit up to 5 x $300,000 writers pretty quickly.
5. We like the people we're going into business with.

Simple rules. Every time we break one, we end up with all sorts of issues, every time we follow the rules we hit wild success. These don't have to be your rules, but in the absence of using these, have some rules and stick to them over time.

CHAPTER 24: WHO PAYS THE BILLS?

Remember this: Who pays the bills — your competitors or your customers? It's your customers, so focus all the time on the customers and what you are doing for them. It's all that matters. I have no visual of my competitor because I am my own greatest competitor. Focus on the customer. Period. Said. Done.

You have two choices in business. Jim Collins, in his fascinating book *Beyond Entrepreneurship*, introduced me to the terms "role model" and "common enemy approach." Here's my view.

Common enemy – When all you want to do is take out your competitor, you become focused on them. This is unhealthy if you can tell me more about them and what they're doing than what you're doing. In fact, you are so consumed that, in essence, you become overly reactive. It works for a while and can really help you to build your business but never in the long term.

Role model – best on the ground. This is the business that's found its space. It's really focused on the clients' unmet and unsatisfied and unidentified needs. You are so focused on improving the customers' condition through your customer journey that you are seen as the role model in the industry that others aspire to be. It's a highly powerful position to be in and it holds you to a high standard.

Always focus on the customer, never on the competitors.

CHAPTER 25: FINANCIAL FITNESS IS A RESOURCE AND RESOURCES BRING CHOICES AND GIVE YOU THE FUEL TO ACHIEVE YOUR POTENTIAL.

In the early days, I used to feel guilty for charging my clients, but now I love it. Making a profit is not an option in business; it's an absolute requirement because it gives you the resources to provide even better products or services.

As a former accountant, I follow some simple rules:
1. Income must be greater than expenses. If income is not greater than expenses, then you're in trouble.
2. You must have multiple sources of income—think passive income interest from money in the bank, rent from property owned, dividends from shares in business and active income and money you get from work. If you have multiple sources, you'll have a great life and reduce your risk.
3. Pay all bills every week by 8pm, Friday.
4. Set a minimum amount that you have to have in your account and work to that. This expands out to a simple theory about how your relationship with money changes the way you think.

How much does it cost you to live a month? Let's say it's $10,000. I have a theory that you need to have 3 times that, so $30,000, in your bank at all times so that you feel safe. If you don't, then you'll exhibit the following behaviours:

Scarcity leads to fear, doubt, uncertainty, poor behaviour and no routine.

Fly above that level and you'll make better decisions. What I then do is I manage to that level. Once I've paid all bills and all credit cards to zero every Friday at 8pm, with anything left over and above, I pay off the mortgage in extra mortgage repayments.

It keeps you paying to the level and sets you on a path to financial freedom.

The next level is comfort which is 6 times your monthly, which is $60,000 and then we get to entrepreneurial, which is 10 times. So that's having $100,000 on hand at any time. Every time you're at 10 times your monthly, I bet you exhibit the following behaviours: Abundance, which leads to strength, confidence, certainty, good behaviour and routine.

I know which space I'd rather be playing from. As your business and your life grow, so too will your monthly, so check in regularly and stick to the plan.

CHAPTER 26: TRUE NET WEALTH MATTERS.

It's a simple thing, but who teaches you about money and finances? I'm a sceptic by nature, but I follow some simple rules. One of those is your true net wealth figure.

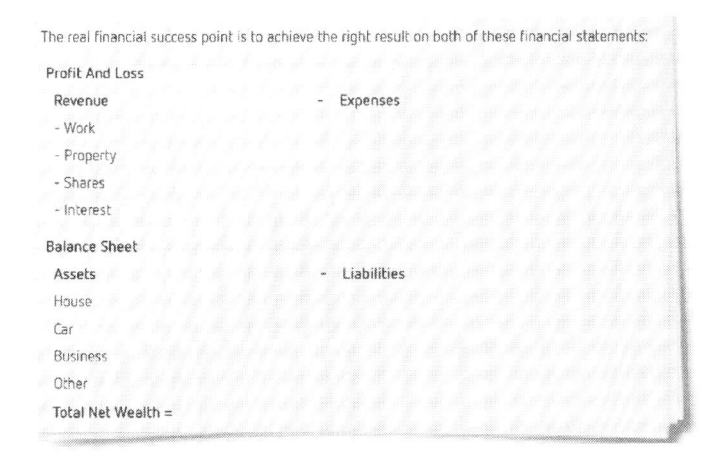

The real financial success point is to achieve the right result on both of these financial statements:

Profit And Loss

Revenue	- Expenses
- Work	
- Property	
- Shares	
- Interest	

Balance Sheet

Assets	- Liabilities
House	
Car	
Business	
Other	
Total Net Wealth =	

Rarely in life is it an expenses problem. As your income rises, so too will your lifestyle. Understand there is a difference between lifestyle assets (which improve the quality of life) and income assets (which produce you income). Your role is to find more ways to increase your value. If you increase your value to the marketplace, you increase your income. To do that, you must always be growing. To become more valuable, you must expose yourself to new ways of thinking, to new experiences. A mind altered and stretched by a new experience can't go back to its old dimensions.

CHAPTER 27: RELATIONSHIP FITNESS.

You talk to you more than anyone else talks to you; so, if you don't like what's being said, change the conversation. Relationships should be the key to renewal, not the key to driving you crazy.

You decide whom you have relationships with and how you interact with others. My goal is to have relationships that are mutually beneficial.

Your relationship with you matters the most, as it will be reflected in every other relationship; in fact, it will be amplified. If you can't look after yourself, you can't look after others; it's that easy.

I have three guiding principles that help me in times of indecision:
1. Health – It always comes first. If you don't have that, you can't do anything else.
2. Family – They matter as they are your greatest supporters; if you work it correctly, they're also the greatest source of renewal and encouragement.
3. Business and career – work provides meaning. Let's face it: you spend your most alert and waking hours at work, so you want to do something that you can learn to love.

I place those appointments in my diary in that order, from health to family and from family to business, not the other way around.

I'm also a believer that the quality of time matters more than the quantity of time. One Christmas, I gave my family 45-minute sessions with me. If they behaved well, I'd give them another 45 minutes. You should have seen how much fun we had, how engaged people were, how the topics remained positive, how we walked away from that family meeting with our tanks full, ready to take on the world.

Mindset matters here, so I don't watch TV or read the news. Tim Ferris was a big influence with his low-information diet of 'only read what you have to.' Get rid of CNN - the constantly negative news. I also love the idea of 'kill the ANTS,' the automatically negative thoughts. We all have them and you can do something about them. Know that you will fight resistance every day. Every day, that voice will tell you no, you don't have to, you don't feel like it. Remember when that happens to kill the ants, say "next" and move on. Put some music on and get on with it.

It's the same with social media. You only live once, so make sure you spend 15 hours a day on the Internet desperately seeking the validation of strangers. Please ask this simple question: "Will this or won't this help me to get me where I want to go?" And if the answer is "No," don't do it.

Partner

What's important to me is to think in the long term rather than being short term and allowing for big compromises to happen. You have one life, so make sure that you live one that you'd re-live if you could.

The loneliest people are those who are in relationships and don't want to be. Here are my thoughts on what's ideal.

Take eight weeks a year on holiday, four weeks with your partner and four weeks on your own. It allows you to explore and see new things together through shared experiences but also independently, so you can be both independent and interdependent. It builds a stronger relationship in the end.

Think; if your relationship is going to last the distance of 50 years or more, I hope you're going to manage your energy, grow your skills and become more interesting.

What I hate seeing is when people grow apart because one is growing and the other is not. I see it happen over and over again, where couples come together in a spectacularly fast fashion, only to divorce a few years later because they never understood or aligned themselves on a bigger future beyond the immediate and they never worked on their values or their relationship.

If you want a relationship to be dynamic, you have to work at it. Think about it; it takes two to tango. Why is it that when people get divorced, they then get fit? It makes it seem like it's okay to be in a relationship and not be fit.

Remember this; the most attractive quality of any human being is someone who's really confident in his or her own skin.

CHAPTER 28: BUSINESS MATTERS.

The key to all great business relationships is this: provide value first and invoice second. Move the free line in your business; that's where you provide great value and do it well before you even send the invoice.

The greatest way to work with your customers is to understand them. Find out about their challenges and their needs, both the unmet and sometimes even the unidentified. Do that and they'll refer you because they find you super valuable.

People like people who are:
1. Relevant – to them and their situations.
2. Frequent – Relevance determines frequency.
3. Consistent – People who turn up on time every time and show up more than just physically.

Be interested. It's the secret to all great relationships. Get off your phone, out of the office, get face-to-face where it matters, share a meal, have a water, be connected. Your network is equal to your net wealth. Grow it every way, every day.

A final thought here: we have thousands of friends on Facebook, connections on LinkedIn and followers on Instagram, but the reality is that none of this matters. What matters is who you share your most intimate dreams, desires, hopes, ambitions and aspirations with because they are the helpers that will hold you to high account and do everything to help you achieve your potential.

Some basic rules:

Set expectations early – what do you both want out of the relationship? Where is there common ground? What are the rules and the values?

Communicate — Short, early conversations save a lot of work. If you get a feeling, communicate it early; don't let things fester.

Be low maintenance — Don't sweat the small stuff; realise that time together is a gift and if you don't get it, it's cool. Independence is a great thing. Don't be needy; keep it fresh. Set time aside for special occasions. You should look forward to date night. Have a family calendar where everything family goes, as it just makes things a lot easier and, plus, you can be cheeky every so often and click maybe on that date night invitation.

Know when you're done. When a relationship has run its course, be thankful that it happened and move on. Cut clean; that doesn't mean you should not be supportive, but don't lead people on. If it's really what you want, set yourself and them free — it really is best for both of you. It's easy to wind yourself in and much harder to wind yourself out.

CHAPTER 29: RECOVERY IS THE KEY TO KEEPING FRESH.

You're going ratchet up the running gear and run a full pace, so it's important you know how to slow down, to rest and recover. Think about it this way: if you are out there stressing and expending, then you need time when you are renewing and resting.

Just like a computer, you need time off and away from the grid. In a super-connected world, that's hard to do, but there are some things you can do to settle:

1. Turn your phone to "do not disturb" mode as soon as you get home. I also play the same music track on my drive home, so I know I'm coming in to land.
2. Meditate every day. A simple app called One Giant Mind is great for that. I try to do it first thing and last thing every day; it keeps me present and in the moment.
3. Realise you need time for yourself, away from everyone else. That thinking time is critical.
4. Every 4 - 6 weeks, have something to look forward to; it keeps you fresh and goal-focused. Get back on the radar of your goals more often.
5. Schedule your recovery. I'm a massive planner and follow my routine. Saturdays are really important for me. I start early with filming my coaching videos with my video team, head straight to recording the podcast with Alexander Phillips, then to a group fitness class called TRX with my personal trainer, Marin. It's an awesome reset and lots of fun. Then, I head to the sauna for 30 minutes. It sucks up all of the water my body is holding and forces me to take time away from all of my

gadgets. I then head into a cold shower before heading off for a one-hour massage. Depending on my schedule, I keep in tune by taking a leisurely afternoon walk, listening to podcasts, working on projects, or catching up with great people. There's no work after 4 p.m. on Saturdays or Sundays unless I really have to push the edges.
6. I prefer to be in bed early on Saturday so that I can run early Sunday. It's the one selfish thing I do to keep me at my best.

Every year, I also go to the Kangaroo Island Health Retreat with Sue McCarthy; she's an oracle. She can see things and fix things that modern medicine can't. She's an asset and I'm glad to have her on my side. At the retreat, we do not use electronic devices and we fast for one week. Under her supervision, a normal day goes like this:

5.30 a.m. Shot of Epsom salts and tea trees oil
6.00 a.m. a short, six-kilometre walk to get the blood flowing
7.00 a.m. Sauna for an hour
8.00 a.m. Thai chi, pilates and stretching
9.00 a.m. Fifteen-kilometre walk on the beach in soft sand
10.30 a.m. Handstands and wading in the water
12.00 p.m. Short rest at the camp
2.00 p.m. Massage and treatments
3.00 p.m. Lecture on nutrition and life
5.00 p.m. Sauna for an hour
6.00 p.m. Biking for an hour
7.00 p.m. Chat back at the camp

During the day, we have little to no food and eight litres of water at room temperature. After a big year on the road, it resets me and my mum tells me it makes me an even nicer person.

Why do I do it? Because after running a year on adrenalin and cortisol, it's nice to return to your natural state. All the bad habits that creep in as you ramp it up get reset.

The mind is the master, the body is the vehicle and practice is the key. – Sue McCarthy

Every year, I also like to spend four weeks attending international conferences or holidaying on my own. It's a great time to confront yourself on where you're at, to catch up on reading, to create new ideas and discover new experiences. I highly recommend it. If you can't spend time by yourself, you can't spend time well with others; you have to be the life of your own party.

CHAPTER 30: PRODUCTIVITY HACKS.

How do you get more done with less? I'm a big believer in systems, because a replicable process produces the same results.

> Simple is scalable. If it works on my mobile, it works everywhere I go. I use the notes section on my phone for everything. All contacts go in contacts; whenever I need a piece of information, I photograph it.

1. Work in 45-minute sessions; it keeps you focused.
2. Write it down. If you need to do it and it's time-limited, add it to your calendar.
3. Each day's events, like calling people, belong in your calendar.
4. Use agendas. I have an agenda for every little meeting I head into with my staff and suppliers. Each agenda is specific to them and they get the agenda well prior. It allows them to be prepared, so we are not walking into a meeting wondering what we are going to discuss or what our contribution is supposed to be.
5. Schedule everything. I put in my holidays 12 months in advance, so I always know how things work. I work to a routine in everything I do. Emotions go to the side pretty quickly. Emotions precede action, yet when we undertake the action, it changes our emotions.
6. Always be on the hunt for new systems. We love tech like Slack.com for teams comms, 15Five for the pulse of our company, Pocket to collect great news stories to read, One Giant Mind for meditation and the Nike Running App to keep my kilometers logged. I also love iA Writer for writing and the Gmail suite for calendar and mail.
7. Always diarise your follow up. When speaking with a client, always

ask them, "Based on that, when should we meet next? What are the next steps?"

8. Book your calendar solid. I am a big believer in holiday when you holiday and work when you work. The worst is when you see someone who's at work on holiday, or even worse, someone who's on holiday while working.

9. Re-read every email before you send it. Once sent, it's super-hard to retract. Make sure you read it and thin it out. Keep it simple. I like to think, "Keep it short." http://two.sentenc.es/ is a great website that promotes the idea of two-sentence-or-less email replies. Anything else should be done through a phone call or a face-to-face meeting.

10. Be direct when you communicate. Don't leave it up to others to figure out what you want.

11. Use emojis in your communication; they add an emotional response.

12. Always take a notebook and a pen to every meeting so that you can take notes and participate. When you arrive, put your phone away, get off social media and be present.

One of the great secrets is to use the "know, feel, do" technique.

When I communicate this message, what do I want the client to:

- Know – a key piece of information or emotional context.
- Feel – Emotional understanding; a viewpoint.
- Do – A specific action.

This led to me using my senses, thoughts and feelings when delivering feedback. It's a great way to get people on the same page.

My sense is that this is like a sixth sense, a deeper insight that I'm about to deliver.

My thoughts are – this is a specific, thought-out set of actions.

My feelings - this is an emotional response to the situation.

When communicating a message, I'll add these at the start of each sentence to deliver in in a way it can be understood and accepted.

Systems are a big thing in everything we do; here's a low-down on what systems you'll need:

1. Checklists. There are two types of checklists: a read-and-review checklist and a read-and-do checklist. A read-and-review checklist is a list of

ingredients you'll need to make the pancakes, like milk, an egg and plain flour. A read-and-do checklist then states the order you need to do them in, i.e. sift the flower, crack the egg, add the milk, whisk briskly, then put in the fridge for 20 minutes before cooking.

2. Forms. These are essential. It's where you capture information in a specific order for later use. In real estate, think of a market appraisal form, listing form, open-for-inspection form, buyer feedback form, making-an-offer form, offer-and-acceptance form, price reduction form, etc. Get the right forms in place and take your people through the form so everything is in its right place.

3. Visuals. These are the key elements of storytelling and storytelling is what selling is all about. The listing presentation really is the ultimate story of what it is that you do for the client. The best visuals are the ones that look real. Case studies, brochures, recent sales, a list of your last 20 sales and your report card on your career history are all great examples.

4. Dialogue – Simple dialogues win. You need to be a person first and a real estate agent second, but with the right dialogue I can take you from zero to hero pretty quickly. My favourite dialogues cut to the chase.

> So, think: is it a checklist, a form, a visual, or a dialogue? If you do that every time something doesn't go to plan, you'll build an incredible business that is teachable. Check out Atul Gawande's fascinating book, *The Checklist Manifesto*.

> I work at a high intensity when I work. Truly, when I'm on stage, there is nothing else going on in the world; I'm focused on my client and helping them to achieve their potential. Focus when you focus.

CHAPTER 31: IF YOU ARE GOING TO USE IT, YOU NEED TO BE EFFECTIVE.

Phone technique matters. I'm flown around the world to help people get better on the phone. Here are some of the key lessons learned:

1. Whatever happens in the first 15 seconds determines the success of the call. You need to be confident and super direct. Time is money and money is time. "Hi Hannah, it's Josh Phegan calling, the reason for my call is..." or "The purpose of my call is..." By clearly stating your purpose, you make it easy for the client to respond.
2. No phone call can be longer than two minutes, unless it is a meeting. If it is longer, you are putting yourself in the position of talking the client out of a face-to-face. You are at your best when you are face to face, that's when you are at your most influential.
3. The customer asks these three questions when you call: who's calling, why are you calling and what does it have to do with me? Answer those three things in the first 15 seconds.
4. When finishing the call, always get the follow up right - where to from here? How can I help you from here? What are the next steps? When should we speak next? Get a clear timeline for follow up, so things don't get weird.
5. Smile before you dial; people can hear it and it matters.

Get a great headset; it frees up your hands so that you can take notes and do what you need to do to convert.

CHAPTER 32: CONSISTENCY MATTERS.

If you market to your customers every quarter, you give them four opportunities a year to put their hands up and say, "I need help." When you market to them every month, it's 12 times and if you do it every week, you have 52 times to engage them.

Now, it's not just volume; relevancy matters:

I've built a business by layering, or adding one thing at a time. I learned to write and be punchy about it, by:

1. Writing a daily email: Every day, for seven years, I've sent a daily email to my key clients. It's kept me fresh, super-relevant and creative.
2. Every week, I send a weekly coaching video. I record a few in advance and I've never missed a week.
3. Then, we added a monthly growth leadership and management tip, which we send every month to business owners.
4. On top of that, we began producing a weekly podcast with Australia's number-one agent, Alexander Phillips.
5. In addition, I make a minimum of 50 connected calls every day.

Put a content calendar in front of you and become obsessive about delivering the value that makes your business great. I know that if I commit, I go all in. If I don't, I don't go all in. It's that simple.

Too many people put their toe in the water just to back down.

CHAPTER 33: THE COMPETITOR DOESN'T PAY THE BILLS.

Why focus on them? I once had a client say do you think that video will take off? What? YouTube and Netflix aren't convincing enough? But my competitor uses video, so I'm not going to.

That's cool. I heard they use the phone, too, so maybe you shouldn't use the phone?

I focus on the one person that matters, the customer. If you become super focused on them, their condition, what you can do for them, how you can anticipate their unmet, unidentified and unsatisfied needs, you'll have more than a business.

Instead, don't miss. Be known as the hitman in your industry and you do that by knowing a little about a lot, keeping a low profile and thinking through your responses. Don't get too emotional; it's business and you will make mistakes.

CHAPTER 34: WHY DO FEELINGS MATTER? LET'S JUST DO THE DEAL.

I have learned the hard way that life teaches you to be patient. If you really want something, sometimes you have to wait.

The old quote "Good things come to those who wait, but only the things that those in the hustle didn't take" is a simple mantra.

In all situations, there are two things to consider:
Empathy – demonstrating understanding around a situation and its emotional impacts.
Urgency – the timeliness of making things happen, with little regard to anything else.

With a little life experience, it is easy to just roll with urgency, but you understand the emotional importance of situations later on. Often, the clients need to get it out. They need time to tell the story. You desperately want to jump in; it is as if you have seen this movie before and you know exactly how it is going to end. Even though you could just jump in to be effective, you need to let them talk it out.

To demonstrate empathy in situations, take more notes. It forces you to ask better questions and listen to the client. I am a massive note taker; it allows me to connect more with the client and to demonstrate empathy. I still have urgency, but I let the empathy shine through.

CHAPTER 35: WHO YOU ARE BECOMING IS MUCH MORE IMPORTANT THAN WHO YOU ARE.

What would happen if you spent as much time reading and in conversations with people who matter, as you do on social media or watching TV?

We all have 84,600 seconds in a day; it's how we use them that matters.

1. Reading. I was never a big reader, but I learnt from my dad early on that it mattered. Just before I started my business, I read 30 books in 30 days. I learnt to highlight as I read, that I had to read a chapter per sitting and then write out all of the highlights into a concise summary so I could review the notes and quotes for later use. I also have a number of books on the go at any one time; that way, if I'm not in the mood for that particular genre or topic, I can choose something that's more my speed for the day.

2. Conversations. Every year, one of my mentors, Simon Dulhunty, challenges me to spend an hour with a person in every age bracket.

    - 0 - 10 years old is all about what's happening right now.
    - 10 - 20 years is all about who you are and what you've got.
    - 20 - 30 years is about discovering who you are and what you expect.
    - 30 - 40 years is about settling and building some basic assets and wealth.
    - 40 - 50 years is about having a full run at wealth creation.

- 50 - 60 years is about discovering new relationship dynamics as kids leave and, for some, careers come closer to their sunset.
- 60–70 is the time to be active and get out and see the things you haven't seen yet.
- 70–80 is a time about contributing and giving back to the world.
- 80–90 is a time to appreciate your life and the things you have lived.
- 90–100 is about spreading the message to care for others.
- 100+ is about... well, you're an absolute living legend!

As medicine progresses, we will live longer, but what's really important is what you do in the years you have. Make sure you're on purpose all the time.

If you want to get good at a skill, find someone who's already good at it. I have learnt from the best in the business. My business heroes are the clients who showed me more than I could have ever imagined and I helped them become masters at what they did. I look for the best in everything I want to learn. To this end, I go to Amazon.com and type my problem in the search box and it always turns out there's plenty of people who've had the same problems and have already solved them, so I read the best book on the subject.

If a reoccurring problem doesn't have a solution, you have to create the solution. Go out and seek the answers.

Here's some thoughts my mentors have left me with:
1. Have intensity about what you do.
2. Be a great connector; don't spend time in the negative, worrying about competitors or gossiping, it helps no one.
3. Be a great family person and care about the people around you; they matter.
4. Have energy for the spirit; it matters about what you do and how you give back to the universe.
5. Back yourself in; no one else is going to.
6. Have big audacious, ambitious goals that scare you.
7. Work the systems and it'll work everything else out in time.
8. Think about how you make people feel.
9. Always find a way and be creative in your approach.
10. Be grounded and real; it matters.
11. Give back to the world.
12. Spend time on your creativity; it makes you a bright spark.
13. Be an avid reader; it helps you become dynamic.
14. Spend time on self; grow you.

CHAPTER 36: DISCIPLINE AND PERSISTENCE.

If there was one thing that really drives me, it's this; find a way. If you really want something, you will find a way. Randy Pausch presented an amazing speech called *the Last Lecture*, which you'll find on YouTube and what he says in that lecture is that brick walls are there to show you how much you want what's on the other side. This is so true. Will you go through the wall, around it, over it, or under it? Write out all the possible solutions and find a way.

I'm dogged in my approach; I don't take no for an answer. No, to me, means "next option," so I keep exploring to really find a solution. Sometimes, I just ask people this: "What would you like to see happen?" Then, I explain my problem and say, "If you were me, how would you fix it?" They then go about providing a solution and you're done.

Raw energy comes from having a lust for life. Just as in the opening scene from *Trainspotting*, choose what you want. Learn how to influence others. You do this by listening and being super-interested in them and what they're becoming.

> *"I've missed more than 9000 shots in my career. I've lost almost 300 games. Twenty-six times, I've been trusted to take the game-winning shot and missed. I've failed over and over and over again in my life. And that is why I succeed." Michael Jordan*

If it matters, you will find a way. Share more of what you want with more people around you and they will help you achieve it. Be a giver, not a taker: it is the winning formula.

PART 2: THE PEOPLE.

CHAPTER 37: THE CONSIGLIERE.

You rise or fall to the level of the people around you. "Hang out with weird, you'll become weirder," says Tom Peters and it's true. From coming from a small town in Australia to seeing the best of the best earning millions of dollars a year in personal income, I learnt to pace, to run at their speed and more.

The people you have around you are critically important. The bigger the dream, the more important the team. The Godfather movie is one of my favourites. In it, there is a character called Tom Hagen; he's the consigliere and he says, "You don't have to have a lot of clients, you just need to have one with a lot of problems." And it is so true.

In times of indecision, who do you call to talk it out? I prefer it not to be your life partner as they don't need the stress. I choose people who are the best at what they do and can take an objective view. They have all read my goal list, achievements list and lessons learned list, so they know me intimately. They know everything about me and life. I'm a big believer in the rule that, if you don't want it on the front page of the newspaper, then don't do it; it's that simple.

I speak with my consigliere every week for around 15 minutes or in times of challenge. They guide me back to true north and keep me focused on achieving my potential and playing the bigger game.

CHAPTER 38: THE MASTERMIND.

I learnt early that you can't always get the people you want in the room, but what would happen if you could create a virtual boardroom? Who's the best person on the ground for marketing, finances, sales, lead generation, social media, relationships, structuring debt, real estate acquisitions, auction day strategy, employing people, etc.?

I have a list of the who's who in my mind for each of those areas and every time I'm thinking "what do I do in this situation?" I just think, "what would they do?"

The skilful ones are the ones who can see things from a different perspective to clearly articulate whether it's a part of the bigger future and whether it should be pursued. When you know what you want at the top of the mountain, your personal Everest, every other decision from that point becomes so much easier. Will it or won't it get me to where I want to go?

CHAPTER 39: TORMENTORS.

A coach is someone who teaches you a very specific skill.

Mentors never give you the answer; they just keep asking the question until you discover the answer for yourself.

Tormentors push you beyond your comfort zone and shake you to your very core to get you moving well past what you thought you'd ever achieve.

The more tormentors in your life, the better. Spend time searching out people who know how to play the bigger game. Meet with them face-to-face, explain and articulate your problems and wait to see the questions that they ask. Some of my best tormentors didn't even know they were doing that for me; they were just the best in that way of thinking and by hanging out with them, they helped me think a different way.

Ultimately, people hang around you because of the way you make them feel. The way you think matters because it creates the conversations and the questions that change your life.

You are where you are right now based on the answers you've given to the questions you've been asked. So either change your answers or ask new questions.

CHAPTER 40: KEEPING BALANCED.

There are three people you want to accumulate in your life:

1. The positive. Every time something goes wrong, ring these people. They are the eternal optimists and will get you moving fast.
2. The negative. Every time you feel that you are flying and that you're the best in the world, ring these people. They'll bring you straight back to earth.
3. The negotiator. Every time you're doing a high-stakes negotiation, ring these people. They'll guide you through the negotiation.

CHAPTER 41: POLARITY.

Although we may be male or female in gender, there is something called polarity and it's possible to have different polarities in different situations.

Let's say a boyfriend and girlfriend are going for a drive on their first date. The boyfriend is driving and suggests that they should go out for dinner.

The girlfriend agrees. He asks, "Where would you like to go?" And she says, "Oh, I'm not sure. Where would you like to go?" And before you know, it goes back and forth, back and forth and no one wants to make the decision.

She doesn't want to say anywhere in case it positions them at the wrong level; he doesn't want to say anywhere because he wants to look consultative. So, before you know it, they return home and he drives off; the relationship is done because they just didn't work it out.

Instead, what actually happened here is that both of them had female polarity.

Male polarity is all about making decisions.
Female polarity is all about the emotional context and wonder of the decision.

I spend the entire day on stage, making decisions for all of my clients: what time we'll break, what exercises we'll do and what conversations we'll have. I've used up all of my male polarity, so when I get home, I switch to female polarity. The last thing I want to do is make any decisions.

The best way to play with it is this: I don't have to be in control, but in the absence of anyone else being in control, I'll be in control.

Playing that situation out looks more like this: Would you like to go for dinner? Yes.
Any particular places you've got on your short list? No.
Ok, cool, so are you feeling more Italian or Japanese? I'm not sure.
Ok, cool, Japanese it is, then.

So, you are consultative yet firm and it keeps everyone happy. If the response was "Yes, I'd like to go to this restaurant," then the polarity has shifted. "Okay, great. Let's go there, then."

Then, you switch to female. What's really important here is that one has to play the male and the other the female and if there's a switch, you must adapt fast, or you will be headed for an argument about things that really don't matter.

It is exactly the same when dealing with high-stake negotiations, working in teams and growing a business.

CHAPTER 42: FAMILY.

Your mother and father are everything. They brought you into this world and, above all, they have defined a lot the values and beliefs that you have carried with you throughout your life.

Things will change, you'll go through stages where you'll be resentful at them and, in the end, you'll wish that you had had more time with them.

It's really important that you work on that relationship all the time. I'm very close to my parents and speak with them most days. They've always been supportive and are now proud of whom their children have become. They gave their best to us, so we must do our best for them.

Heal any relationships that are broken and that are important to you. When they're gone, you'll wish you had taken the advice.

PART 3: SYSTEMS.

CHAPTER 43: GETTING CONSISTENT RESULTS.

You will measure your life based on the experiences you get to have and the people you get to share them with. So, to do more, you must become more. To do this, you will need a system for growth. Here's what I've used to rapidly drive success.

Step 1: Inputs:
Show me your library (books, podcasts, conversations) and it will show me your bank account.

Inputs matter; they determine your outputs. What you read, listen to and interact with determines the person you become. There's no doubt that the fastest way to learn is to think; someone has already mastered the skills that you want to become great at. Find out who they are and follow them; get in touch and learn from the best.

For every skill that you want to master, find your master. I've got an insatiable appetite to grow and learn as much as I can. The day you stop learning is the day you stop evolving and there's no doubt that you will have better relationships and a better life when you bring a better conversation to the game. Nobody likes boring; everybody likes mysterious, intriguing, well-thought-out and well-executed.

Reading matters. The problem is that I need a system for it. I didn't love it and, more often than not, I fell asleep during it. So, how do I read now?

1. I always have more than one book on the go at any one time. It's awesome because, if I don't feel like reading one book, I can read another. This lets me jump from heavy topics to light fiction to non-fiction.
2. When I read, I keep a highlighter in hand, or if I'm on a Kindle, I highlight as much as possible. When I'm done with the book, I type up my highlights or export them from the Kindle online app into a document. This becomes the source of great quotes and ideas the shape the type of person I want to become. Even better, I now have a summary of great books to read. I read a lot now and I keep the "best of the best" books on hand for my team.
3. When new staff members join me, I give them a list of books to read to make them the very best they can be. Plenty of people don't read anymore and they should. Reading can get other people on our wavelength and it keeps us dynamic. If you want to be a leader, you must go out there and seek; otherwise, you'll be a manager, doing what you do with only the limited information you already have.
4. I'm not a lover of audio books; I find that people fall asleep or become distracted quickly, then end up doing something else.
5. Podcasts are the new library for learning. Some incredible interviews and soloists share the latest and greatest on any topic you could imagine.
6. I don't listen to commercial radio or watch commercial TV. Why would I? I've never spent an hour watching them and then thought, "Wow, that was an awesome way to spend an hour!" The constantly negative news (CNN) is rarely going to help me to achieve my goals. I only watch, listen, or read things that will help me in my pursuit to achieving my potential.
7. Conversations are still king. You rise or fall to the level of the people around you. Constantly upgrade your conversations and hang out with diverse people from other industries and countries and you will grow. I love to travel at least two weeks every year to a non-English-speaking country to push my development, appreciation and communication skills.
8. YouTube and TED talks are awesome, but the best videos, documentaries, books, podcasts and webinars will be the ones you create yourself. It's exploring your experiences and knowledge that allows you to achieve new personal growth.

Step 2: Environment. Setup your environment so that it supports the type of person you want to become. – Clate Mask.

There I was at a conference in America, listening to the CEO of Infusionsoft, Clate Mask, talk about the importance of your environment. Setting up your environment matters for long-term success.

The negative mirror.

Imagine you have a tough boss and every day for 30 days, you come home and tell your partner about how demanding your boss is and how he or she never recognises your achievements or helps you out. Then, one day, you come home and tell your partner how amazing your boss is and how he or she is the best person you've ever worked for.

What happens? Your partner doesn't react the way you expect. They remind you how bad your boss was over time and not to expect any lasting change in the new behaviour. And that's exactly what happens to us in life: the more we communicate to others about a situation, the more they will back us in our beliefs. Before you know it, there's too much resistance for change to take effect.

The challenge is that we use those closest to us to keep us level. The best thing to remember is that your partner is around you because you bring the fun and adventure to life as no one else does. So be careful with the role you play. To keep level, consider having three people in your life apart from your life partner.

The positive person – this person is super positive. Every time something goes wrong or you need a pick-me-up, ring this person first.

The negative person – every time you feel like you're flying, like you own the world, ring this person; they'll bring you straight back to the ground and keep you humble.

Negotiator – Whenever you're negotiating, always have a third party to take the negotiation past an impasse.

None of these are salaried positions; they are just great people willing to help you to achieve your potential. Whatever you put in, you get back. Remember to be there for them, too, when they need you because that is what builds great relationships.

Step 3: Attitude.
Your attitude determines your altitude. My school library.

I was looking around my school library one day when I saw a sign that said, "Your attitude determines your altitude." I thought it was funny and they had spelt attitude wrong the second time. I had to look up altitude in the dictionary.

Ivan Bresic said to me some time ago, "Every person you meet has a tattoo on their forehead; make me feel important, remember that." So, everywhere I go, I smile and engage with people. I choose to hold the door open and bring positive energy to the table.

There are four steps to building an invincible attitude in life:

1. Coach
The difference between a coach and a mentor is that a coach teaches you a very specific skill. They are there to teach you how to kick the ball through the goal. They look at specific tried and tested methods to help you achieve a specific outcome. You need a lot of coaches in your life if you want to perfect a lot of skills. Who are your coaches?

2. Mentor
Mentors are brilliant because they ask you questions but never provide answers. They ask the questions that get you to come up with the answers. When you are a part of the change, you don't resist it. When change happens to you, you do. Mentors help you to achieve much loftier goals than you ever thought you could.

3. Inspire
These people you don't even need to know. They are individuals that are where you want to be, or exhibit behaviours you seek as desirable. They don't even have to be alive, to drive inspiration for what you want to achieve in life.

4. Lead
Leaders are different than managers. Managers manage to the level; they never achieve new ground, rather they uphold to the existing level. Leaders discover new frontiers and they are prepared to ask the questions and are dissatisfied easily but seek our new solutions better known as a bigger future; they also know the vision for success and they are prepared to make the first steps.

To be brilliant, have someone in each of these areas for your life to ensure your attitude is at it's best. Real growth comes when you realise you need to be each of those for others. The leadership position is where all great growth happens in your life.

Step 4: Behaviours: Our attitudes shape our behaviours.

Behaviours are what we do. If our attitude is right, our behaviours will follow. In everything I do, I ask myself if it would be okay if it ended up on the front page of the newspaper tomorrow morning. Am I playing in the leadership position, or am I compromising what I really want in life because I'm not playing to the standard of what I'm capable of?

Here are some behaviours that will make you super-efficient.
1. Cut to the chase. No phone call is to be longer than two minutes unless you're booking an appointment. We know that in the first 15 seconds, we can tell if someone really wants to talk to us or not. You are at your most influential when you are in front of people; talking over the phone is a close second and everything else is a distant third. Be efficient in what you do. Think about who, why and what. When someone answers a call, they think, 1. Who is calling? 2. Why are they calling me? and 3. What does it have to do with me? Answer those efficiently and you will experience more success.
2. Make outgoing phone calls in 45-minute sessions. We know that the body works in 90-minute cycles, better known as your circadian and ultradian rhythms. They are the reason you sleep when it's dark and stay awake when it's light. They are the reason why when you turn off your alarm and go back to sleep for another 10 minutes, you feel more tired than if you had just got up when your alarm went off initially. You are now 10 minutes into the next cycle and it will take the balance of the 90 minutes to fully wake up. We have done thousands of call sessions around the world and find that 45 minutes is long enough for impact and short enough to maintain momentum. During a 45-minute session, we know you will need 16-24 names and numbers to call. 50% of all the calls you make will end up in voicemail and 50% will be answered. Of those that are answered, if you are good, you will get a 33% conversion rate. The warmer the lead, the higher the conversion. I choose to only work with people who know they are dissatisfied, have a vision for what they see as the solution and are prepared to make more first steps than others.
3. When leaving a voice mail, I only ever leave my name and number. "Hi Hannah, it's Josh calling, can you call me back? +61 448 406 303." It's killer. It's direct, drives up anxiety and curiosity in the client and gets them to call you back. If you leave all the detail, including the firm you're calling from, the customer has the chance to opt out. You may have some game-changing questions or information that

changes the whole game, though and you'll never have the chance to present them.
4. Effectiveness matters. Success in prospecting is getting face-to-face with your customers; that's where all the magic happens. I work to three appointments booked per call session. If you can do that, you'll write your million dollars and some. Three appointments a day should lead to 15 a week and 60 a month. Review your calendar, get honest with yourself and count your appointments. I use a simple system to label all of my appointments, which makes it really easy to search and report. Use a three-letter identifier followed by a space and a dash; then, you can search and get your numbers:

LAP - Listing appointment
MAP - Market appraisal appointment
BAP - Buyer appointment
OFI - Open for inspection
PSM - Pre-settlement meeting
AUC - Auction

If you really want success, you have to understand what that looks like for you. Is it more important that you get the job done or that you are in attendance from 9 a.m. to 5 p.m.? Great question!

The second question that really helps here is, "I have a financial plan. I know that you guys have a financial budget and I just wanted to see how close your financial budget is to meeting my financial plan." People hate that question, but it makes things real. If you want to hit your target, you have to have one and more importantly, you need to know what sort of value you need to bring to the table so that whoever is managing you is considered highly successful because you are on the team.

CHAPTER 44: YOU HAVE TO GROW.

Mark Zuckerberg isn't coding all of Facebook himself and neither should you. If you want to scale, you have to build a team around you.

The easiest way to do this is by performing work where you really add value. A simple exercise works like this.

Hate: Write out a list of all the things you hate doing that someone else could do at a lower dollar value than you're worth.

Not great: Write out a list of all the things that you feel not great about doing. Are they things that are essential to your role, or could you get other people to do them for you? You either build the skill or you hire it.

Love: What are all the things that you love to do? How can you do more of them, more often?

Measure things out of 5, 1 being it's not important to me, to 5 being it's super important to me, anything below a 4 outsource it. I love buying fresh food for my house; it's a 5, so it stays; I'm not super passionate about washing and ironing my work shirts; so, it goes.

You have to let go to grow. Here are the reasons why people don't let go:

1. They love doing it and don't want anyone else to get the enjoyment.
2. Trust issues - you don't trust the people on your team.
3. You're not prepared to train others, or you don't have the time to do it.
4. You are convinced you are a unicorn and no one else can do it, so it's

a unique skill that you haven't built a system for yet.
5. You don't want someone else to get the credit for it because your ego won't let that happen.
6. You lack the vision. This is the most dangerous one. Most people I see in small business lack vision; that's why they're lonely. It's your job to build and maintain the vision in everything you do.

CHAPTER 45: RESULTS. IF IT DOESN'T MATTER WHO WINS OR LOSES, THEN WHY DO THEY KEEP SCORE? – VINCE LOMBARDI.

What does success look like for you? How will you know when you've achieved it? For real estate agents, the numbers are simple. Appraisals, listings, sales and income.

Which of the four is the most important? Income. It's always income. And which one is the greatest indicator of future success? Listing. If you've got the stock, you've got the market.

So that's all I focus on. To level up the game, I know consistency counts. By day 7 in the month, I need to be a 1/4 of the way through my target, by day 14, 1/2 way, by day 21, 3/4 of the way and by day 28, I have to hit the target.

I see a lot of people surge in business. They have this late run every month. It is as if they love the thrill of the pressure in the last week of the month, or in the last month of the year to try and hit their numbers.

If I want to win, I stay consistent. And just like watching Olympic swimmers try to smash the Olympic record by staying ahead of the world record line, so too do we.

The most important measure of success are holidays. They keep you fresh, focused on your goals, get you away from the game and help you to keep sharp by providing you with new experiences. The more holidays you can have, the better your business. People who don't holiday are often proud of this; this view is not for me. I much prefer to holiday often. Every six weeks, you need something out in front of you that keeps you focused. I plan my holidays 12 months in advance, booked and paid for. Holidays are not options.

If you watch your inputs, set up an environment for success, have an attitude of gratitude and find a way to work on your behaviours and know what success looks like (results), you'll achieve more success than you ever thought possible. The challenges for most people are the wrong inputs, a poor environment and an attitude of entitlement (not prepared to do the work), all of which lead to poor behaviour. Most of it really comes down to a lack of vision. Decide what you want and go all out to get it.

CHAPTER 46: FIND A WAY.

Initiative matters. Google will help you go a long way in life; ask more questions, surround yourself with people doing bigger and better things and you'll find a new level.

Every time I'm told no, it forces me to decide what's on the other side of that no. If I really want it, I find a way. I negotiate and that's what you should do, too.

CHAPTER 47: A LITTLE HISTORY WORTH REPEATING: THE SECRET TO BUILDING A WINNING TEAM.

If you want to scale, you have to build a winning team. The truth is, too many people are searching for unicorns. You employ for attitude and you teach skill. The age, profile and demographics of your staff are just as important as the age, profile and demographics of your clients. You want to pair like with like and have a good mix so that all sections of your business work.

Here's the best way to start:

- I love to work with people who I have already worked with in the past. There is an instant trust relationship, you get each other, you know how the other works.
- The funny thing about recruitment is that I meet people in business who claim that there are no good people out there and then I meet great people elsewhere who tell me there aren't any great jobs. Funny, why don't those two just meet? Surely, it's not that hard. So where does your customer hang out before they need you? Customer, but aren't we talking about employees? Yes, exactly, because your employees are actually your customers; they turn up every day and they buy the opportunity to work in your firm. You provide a service, an opportunity to serve and they get to work the systems, experience growth, gain new skills and insights and, most importantly, grow by doing meaningful work.

Here are some great lead sources:

1. Your social profile matters. Write out an awesome list of all the benefits of what it's like to work in your business. I like all the benefits beyond the financial. Think about more annual leave, your birthday off work, the latest and greatest in equipment, staff trips for planning meetings, great dinners and experiences, international travel. Film a short video about it, post it on your social accounts and see what happens. Great people will find you.
2. The reality is that you won't find me on a recruitment website, looking for jobs. Great talent isn't looking for work; they've already got it. Your existing network knows many people who could work for you.
3. I also love it when customers become employees. They love what you do, understand future customers' needs and can deliver the service. Could it be as simple as putting up a "Now Hiring" sign at your place of work and seeing what happens?
4. Develop a talent bench. I'm always recruiting. I'm looking for great people who are doing amazing things. I find a way to interact and stay working on it. When I see people I like, I become their friend and work those relationships until the day I find something for them to do in my business; then, I strike.

I'm a big believer in the idea that we get the wrong people in business because we don't follow simple systems. Here are a few things to consider:

1. An application form: You can find some awesome ones online. Get all the information you want in the right order so you can compare candidates. When you employ someone, you also get all of his or her network, so if that employee knows other great talent, it will open brand-new doors for you.
2. Check their social accounts; it tells you a lot about them. Find out how many friends and followers they have. Remember the rule: if you wouldn't want it on the front page of the newspaper, you don't post it. Do they know that rule?
3. Don't assume. I continue to work on a great list of questions that I ask in every interview. I keep working on them and with every person I employ, I ask the same questions. I've been caught out too many times. I want to know exactly where their skills are. Call me old-school, but if they can't work out 10% of $800,000, then good luck them spotting errors or using maths to quickly work out our profit margin on our products and services.
4. Skill testers matter. I'm a huge fan of Typingtest.com. If they can't type a minimum of 45 words a minute, I don't want them on my team. I'm at 88 words a minute and I want people that can respond fast. We work in a

world where communication matters. I also love the test that Tom Rath has in his best-selling book *Strength Finders 2.0*. You can find out their top 5 strengths, then identify the weaknesses and strengths of each strength are, so you know what you're recruiting for.
5. Make people jump through a few interviews. Once I've got them past the first two, then we go to the third, where I ask them to go and buy the book *Cut to the Chase* by Stuart Levine and then send me the summary. It takes around 2 hours to read. It's amazing how many people don't know where to buy a book, or how to summarise one. If they can't do that, how will they learn?
6. The next step is then to spend a day with me working. I want to see how they work under pressure. If all goes well, I love a meeting with them and their partner over dinner to talk them through what things look like and make sure we have all the expectations on the table.

CHAPTER 48: LETTING GO IS TEACHING PEOPLE HOW TO GROW.

As you speed through life, you forget how many skills you amass. You are rich in history, experiences and perceptions; however, not everyone is the same.

When we look for people to join our teams, we often look for unicorns. It's always the people who aren't right, but what if it's where we source our candidates from, our interview process, or, most importantly, what we do before they join our business that determines all success?

Whatever happens in the first hour, the first day, the first week and the first month is what people think happens in the organisation for the rest of time.

Make it an experience. When you put an offer to someone, make sure it's in writing. Always put the word 'draft' in the top right-hand corner; it gives you negotiation room to make it easy for them to iron out any questions they might have.

As soon as they sign, I hand them a Kindle and on that Kindle I have the books they need to read to be great in that role for my business. I then order their new Apple MacBook Pro and send the receipt to their email address. I set everything up as though they are a part of our company ASAP, so the moment they arrive, they have business cards, access to all our systems and everything they need for success. I love the idea of a welcoming party where you put the cake on first to welcome them to the firm. Why do we always have leaving parties but never arriving parties? It just seems like it's the wrong order.

In my view, the moment someone joins your company, that person is another moment closer to leaving it. It's your job to keep the future exciting and keep building your employees' values so you can progress their careers and grow a great company.

CHAPTER 49: 10 KEY SKILLS AND WHY YOUR APPROACH MATTERS.

What are the 10 key skills you need to teach that will make your new hire super valuable? The quicker you can deem them competent in the skill, the sooner they'll bring value to the firm. I never assume competency regardless of how much perceived experience someone has because that person's way is not my way and my way is what makes my business great.

Here are 10 key skills to be a great agent:
1. Running an open for inspection
2. Opening for inspection callbacks
3. Just listed/sold calls as they happen
4. Database entry
5. Filling out all the forms we use in the business
6. Running successful appointments
7. Running a successful meeting
8. Managing a diary
9. Making an offer
10. Dealing with multiple offer situations

Now that we've got those 10, there are 100 more where they came from. How does someone learn these skills in your organisation?

In reality, it is luck. Hopefully, the new hire will sit next to someone good. Notice that the spare tables in the office are usually not next to the good people, either.

Hopefully, that person will want to take the time to show

the new hire the ropes and hopefully, the new hire will be keen to learn. Now that we're past the miracles you expected, let's talk about what really needs to happen.

We train in short, sharp, 15-minute stints at the same time every day. Mondays through Thursdays, we teach one key skill.

Let's take open for inspections:
Mondays – Where the checklist, pointer boards, flags and keys are
Tuesdays – How to set up the kitchen bench and point of sale materials
Wednesdays – How to use technology, check people in and take names and numbers
Thursdays – Questions around pricing, bathroom use and a million other things

Then, on Fridays, we assess. For 15 minutes, your new hire has to set up the boardroom as though it's an open house and follow a checklist. You'll attend as a buyer and see just how close it comes to standard.

If he or she nails the standard, you can move on to the next skill. If not, review it until you make it. Standards matter in business because they are your brand.

Now that we have a new skill, we take an A4 piece of paper with a big circle on it and call it the circle of competencies. Now, we write that skill inside the circle and place it in the employee's file. We keep adding skills to the circle, building competence and, therefore, confidence.

Imagine if someone had done that when you started your career. How much would that have progressed then? The catch is that we always teach the how but never the why of delivering on standards or why it matters so much to customers.

Reality is a better teacher than you, so the sooner employees can practice, the faster they will learn, the more valuable they will become and the higher the level of work both of you will do.

You want people prepared to invest in their learning and therefore their professional growth. To find them, ask them how they learn after finishing school.

Their answers will tell you a lot about why they're sitting in front of you and what their future looks like if you don't intervene and stop the poor approach to learning.

What we know is that we rush kids from school into universities without any real clue about the jobs for which they're being trained. They have little to no understanding as to what the real world looks like and then they graduate, start working and realise pretty soon that what they trained for isn't what they thought it was. That's why I've met web designers that studied to be physiotherapists but quit once they started working in the real world because they realised they didn't like touching people or nurses who quit working in hospitals because they didn't like seeing patients pass away.

We have a duty to explain to people what success looks like in our business fully. Be proud that the people who join you are never the same after they've met you because they learn how to learn.

CHAPTER 50: MAKE IT EASY ON YOURSELF.

If there is any conversation you need to have more than once, record it on video. Be precise in your communication. Take those videos and add them to an automated system that can email the videos out to your new hires. Make the process easy. You could have videos like the following:
1.   History of the company and why it matters.
2.   Purpose: The job we get done for the customer and why they find that valuable.
3.   Standards in business, the essential ingredients of our brand.
4.   Values - the rules by which we play the game.
5.   The how to, where to and when to of our company.

Make it short, sharp and effective.

CHAPTER 51: CAREER PROGRESSION.

"I didn't know that when I got a job with you that I also got a life sentence. Believe it or not, I actually have aspirations and ambitions greater than just working for you in marketing." April Forbes

She said it and it smashed me hard. My number one, who'd helped me to build this great business in the early days, was leaving. The challenge wasn't that we didn't work well together, nor was it that we weren't growing; it was that my vision wasn't clear on where we could grow and where we could go. It was clear enough for this year but not far out enough. When you deal with highly talented people, they want challenges and problems to solve.

Career progression matters in business, but it often doesn't happen because, in a rapidly growing business, managers struggle to flesh out their organisational charts. If you don't have the chart, you don't have the roles.

Here are some career paths:

Property Management:
Receptionist > Leasing > Junior Property Manager > Business Development Manager > Property Manager > Senior Property Manager > Department Manager > Business Owner

Sales:
Office Cadet > Sales Assistant > Sales Person > Senior Sales Person > Sales Manager > Business Owner

Questions for each role:
1. What are the three key roles that the person needs to perform?
2. What are the key skills that need to be mastered and competencies that need to be demonstrated?
3. At which systems do they need to be proficient? Think forms, checklists, dialogues and visuals.
4. What books do they need to read?

For each of the roles, develop pay scales. Each role fits into a pay level and, in that way, if people want to be paid more, they need to take on more responsibilities, build new capabilities and bring more value to the table.

- Band 5 – $150,000
- Band 4 – $100,000 - $150,000
- Band 3 – $80,000 - $100,000
- Band 2 – $60,000 - $80,000
- Band 1 – $45,000 - $60,000

This prevents you from having a terrorist in your company seeking you out when you are vulnerable and skipping several pay grades in low-level positions. I'm all for paying people what they're worth and I'm even more for people bringing value to the table more often. Build a company that rewards talent, not terrorism.

In the absence of having a clear progression path, you're making it up on the fly and will lose great talent.

Remember to set expectations early and make it clear on how to progress. Offer no pay increases if you haven't read the books. It's worked wonders in teaching people how to learn.

CHAPTER 52: CLARITY ON WHAT MATTERS – THE BIG THREE.

The big three matter. These are your core responsibilities in your role and are what you do 80% of the time.

As the leader of my business my big three are as follow:
1. The vision and direction of the company.
2. Growth in new markets, products and services.
3. On-stage delivery.

If I don't do those well, nothing happens.

Once I've gotten those, I then have my big three for the next year:
1. Web, digital and social strategy.
2. Write the book.
3. New podcast series.

These are larger, chunkier projects that are important to achieving the overall vision.

Then, I break them down into the next quarter. What are the critical things that will help me achieve my annual or overall goals?

1. New website wireframes.
2. Chapter and content pages for the book.
3. Record the pilot of the new podcast.

Now that you've got that clear, work with the people in your team to do the same for them and their roles. It takes time initially, but once you do it, it provides unbelievable clarity for everyone. You reset, renew and refocus on what's important.

I remind my team often that I've never grown a business this big before, so I will make mistakes, roles will change and people will need to adapt. It's the truth and the truth always sets you free. Cut me some slack and let's grow this thing.

CHAPTER 53: PROSPECTING AT ITS BEST.

Everything you do is prospecting. The secret is to be interested: be interested in people, their stories, what you can do for them and what your business does to solve their problems.

Your personal network is everything in business and you build it from day one. Add every person you meet to your contacts. I like to add people to my phone whenever they call so that I've always got their contact in my phone, so when they ring, I can answer as though we've already done business and that they are important enough to me to put in my phone.

I only work with people I like. Occasionally, you'll meet some people that are a little strange, but don't let their insecurities get in the way of them being a profitable customer in your business. There's a reason they've come to you: what you can do for their future and a better now.

CHAPTER 54: HOW REFERRALS WORK.

Most people don't understand referrals. Here's what works:

1. Never pay for a referral. People should refer you because you are really good at what you do. As soon as people need an inducement to refer you they have their own self-interests at heart, not the interests of person who they've referred. Plus, what happens when the next competitor comes along with a slightly higher referral fee? What will you do then?
2. To get referrals, give referrals. Never accept any referral gifts. A "thank you" is more than enough. Look for opportunities to refer people who are really good at what they do.
3. Deliver on your service. There should be no difference between how you treat a referred lead versus a brand-new or existing lead. Everyone gets the same high standard of service.
4. At all times, keep the referrer in the loop. Treat them as though they are a part of the transaction and communicate with them when you communicate with the end customer. That way, whenever the referrers see the customer, they won't feel awkward as they know exactly where things are.
5. Ask the referrer to check in with the customer often to get a more candid offline review of what you do.

Treat referrers like family. Go out of your way to be a friend, catch up from time to time, thank them consistently and help them where you can, particularly in times of need. I can count every lead I've ever generated back to a handful of key referrers who've helped me build my business.

CHAPTER 55: NO, REALLY, HOW DOES IT FEEL?

What would it be like to be one of your customers? I dare you to put yourself into your database and see what you get from you.

If you feel like you'll spam your audience, then it's time to tighten up, refresh and renew your marketing. We do this every 18 months. That's how fast our business moves; what we thought was good back then is often cringeworthy now.

Add yourself to your database in every category and see what the customer gets. Layout, messaging and mediums matter. Think of these layers:

- Calls
- SMS
- Email - How well does it look on mobile?
- Social - Retargeting and organic posting
- Direct mail
- Signage
- Point of sale materials

Going undercover and testing out your team matters. Mystery shopping is a great way to test the consumer. This is where you send customers in to identify gaps in the service delivery. Just because it worked when you built it does not mean it still works now.

Everything has a purpose and a goal and goals change.

CHAPTER 56: HOW FAT IS YOUR DATABASE?

The challenge is that we get a thrill in chasing the new. There's just something about catching something we've never caught before. In business today, we've become hunters of the right here right now and very rarely do we work on our lead nature campaigns.

The problem is we take the customers' word on their timeline on when they'll be ready, but we really don't understand where they're at, what the problem really is, what their vision for the solution is, or even if they're prepared to make the first steps.

Most clients I work with ask what's the perfect size for their database, as though they'll start marketing to it, or wait for the magic to happen at a critical number. What I know is the perfect number is one. That's all you need, one customer who has a lot of problems for you to solve. The secret is to grow that database beyond one and send it to 1,000. Personal matters, so keep it personal and write all your marketing material to just one customer. It changes your whole perspective.

To get your database fit, look for simple opportunities. To be fit, you have to work it. I look at LinkedIn every day to see who has changed roles; we then update them in our database and send them communications to say congrats on their new role. Every time there's an email unsubscribe there's a reason for it; either the prospect just bought, sold, or moved on. Chances are that someone else unsubscribed for them, so if you call them, you have a chance at catching them.

Every person in your database most likely started out as a buyer, so call from that perspective. Have you found anything?

CHAPTER 57: LANGUAGE MATTERS.

A client calls me and says, "Josh, I need your help. I'm calling all the past clients of the firm and they just don't seem to want to talk. Can you help?"

"Sure, talk me through what you're saying and who are the clients, by the way?"

"They are past clients from my former boss. He passed away a few years ago."

"Sorry to hear. Let's do the call."

"Hi, Hannah. It's Josh calling. You may remember you bought your house from Harry. Well, look, he's died and I just thought I'd check in to see how's the house?"

Stop right there; the customer is more concerned that your former boss has died. That's the blockage. To get super effective with your calls, record them and play them back. If you wouldn't buy from you, don't ever expect anyone else to buy from you. If you don't sound confident on the phone, lift up the volume. Most people are shy when they should be strong and they mumble when they should speak out.

I have a simple rule: If you wouldn't say it in a date, don't say it in the workplace. Here's language that stops people in their tracks:

Database: No one wants to be in your database.
Instead of getting to business straight away,
try to make a personal connection first.

Previous appraisal and market appraisal: I get the point of this, but it's weird. When checking on the progress, ask how things are going, what the next steps are and how you can help?

Private treaty: How many private treaty boards have you seen lately? Not many.

Gold, silver, bronze, platinum, diamond and advantage: Please. The customer knows it as large, medium or small. How many times do you walk into a cafe and they offer you the regular or the medium coffee and you have to look around to find the cups with the labels "Regular" and "Medium" on them?

CHAPTER 58: 80%, SHIP IT.

The reality is that you can work away to get things 100% perfect, but does it really matter? I was a perfectionist when I started. In fact, I held off sending my website live for one year because I couldn't decide if the phone number in the top right corner should be blue or black. One of my good friends April said, "Okay, here we go: Will this decision make the difference as to whether we turnover a million this year or not?" I said, "No, it won't." She said, "Great, it's blue, then."

Like that, the decision was made. That was a life-changing moment. Ship it at 80% and stop letting perfection get in the way. We overcomplicate things. It's better to get Version 1 out the door and test it than wait until you've got it perfect. If it's at 80%, it's customer-ready.

CHAPTER 59: MEET ANDREW.

When I first started, I got really clear on one thing: our customer avatars. I went to work to find out everything about the customers so I'd know how to serve them.

Andrew is a million-dollar writer in the real estate industry. He sells properties in and around King's Cross. His office is located underneath the iconic Coca-Cola sign. He's built a great team of himself, an executive assistant and a junior agent in his team that specialises in working with buyers.

Andrew has an amazing wife at home who is bringing up their two kids under the age of six, so he lives a busy business life. He sells 100 properties a year, mainly via auction and completes around 10 open homes every Saturday. He's focused on delivering great service.

Last week Andrew went for a walk to get some lunch and as he was crossing the street, he was hit by a car. They rushed him down to St Vincent's Hospital for emergency surgery. It turns our everything is ok, except that he now suffers temporary memory loss or amnesia, related to everything real estate. He doesn't know what a contract is, how to run an open, what to do with his team, etc.

Andrew goes to talk to his boss, at which point his boss hands over my business card and says, call this guy, he'll teach you everything you need to know to be a million dollar agent and get you back to doing what you should be doing, fast.

Andrew doesn't exist. He's one of my ideal customers; he's an avatar and every time I write something, I write it to Andrew first. That's how I keep the marketing and content punchy, because if it's written for one, if it's written for Andrew, it's written for all. Clients regularly tell me that they feel like I'm in their head, like I'm just over their shoulder, when in fact all I'm doing is writing to Andrew and as a great avatar, he shares all the same characteristics as they do.

Here are some thoughts on building out your avatars. I have them for all the different types of customers we serve, from those just starting out, to established agents, business owners and CEO's.

The Customer Avatar - The Ideal Customer
What area do they live in? Nominate an area, a postcode, a style of property, a price point.

What's the total income received into their household? This determines their disposable income and how likely they are to be economically driven when selecting an agent, which determines the pitch of your brand.

What's their marital status? Single, divorced, or happily married?

Do they have any kids? What time restrictions does that place if they have a busy family life?

What are their common experiences? Where do they go and what do they do? What do they enjoy and what annoys them?

What brands do they commonly associate with? Are they Nike or Puma, Louis Vuitton or Chanel?

If they went to a shopping centre, which shops/brands would attract them? Are they more for The Reject Shop or a high-end department store, a boutique, or a chain shop?

What brand and model of car do they drive? This tells you their preference towards safety, performance, appearance, convenience, economy, or reliability.

What are their fears? How do they feel about the transaction and what can you do to minimise those fears?

What are their aspirations? Who do they intend to be? What are their hopes, dreams and visions for their lives?

Name the client:

Now, do that for every client type you have and teach that to your people. That's how you make your marketing super relevant. It keeps you customer-focused.

When you go to this level of detail, you start to think about where this customer hangs out. If customers hang out at the local school or the local football team, then it makes sense that that's where you hang out. If they drive a conservative car, then you drive a conservative car.

When you match the customers and their expectations with what you deliver, you have a recipe for success. It also means how and what you post on social media, combined with the quality of the point of sale materials you have on display in the offline world, must match the customers.

This is where brand becomes important. Brand is the promise of what you'll do for the customer and the standard at which you'll deliver on that promise.

Think what you are known for and why that matters.

In the book *Behind the Golden Arches*, Ray Kroc identifies that McDonald's wanted to be known for three key things:

1. Speed of product: How quick from when you order can they get that hamburger in your hand?
2. Cleanliness of the store: It's the brand experience. Make sure the bathrooms are well-serviced and people will keep coming back. If you pay attention to the bathrooms, imagine how much attention people pay to the kitchen.
3. Innovation for the family: It's a family restaurant and innovation is what keeps the customers coming back. Keep adding new flavours but always have the staples. That way, people can rely on you and try out new services, which will actually increase their loyalty.

Remember, the customer is the marketer. If they have a great experience, they come back and bring others. Word of mouth is the fuel in great stories of businesses taking off, but it can set your profit on fire if the experiences are negative.

What are you known for?
Why does the customer find that valuable?
When could your employees raise or fall short of the service standards?
Does everyone in the team know your brand's standards well enough that they can achieve a consistent brand experience?

That's what sets you apart: Getting fit, knowing what you deliver and delivering it consistently.

The marketing positions the brand, the brand determines the fee and the fee creates the brand experience. You probably have a very different view of a budget offering versus a luxury offering. You have to remember that someone else's model is not your model. The client cares more about consistency than your giving 110%.

Getting that clear is all that matters in business. That way, you don't have to recruit unicorns—exceptional talent that's hard to come by. I just want regular people who are hungry to learn and keen to serve.

I never really understood that when I first started. The people around me would always explain how we did things, even when we did them, but what's more important is to explain why we do them. Execution at the right time matters because of what it does for our customers and their condition. You have to know why people find what you do valuable and keep going back to the customers to find those unidentified, unmet and unsatisfied needs. That's what makes you valuable. Your ability to identify those and meet those are the game changers that let you shape your entire industry.

When you teach the why, you teach thinking and innovation. When you treat people like followers, they act like followers. When you treat people like leaders, they'll find the space to be leaders. Managers manage the existing standards, but a leader seeks new experience, finds new spaces to grow and, above all else, gets an organisation into, through and past important periods of change.

I don't have to be in control. I just need to know that someone is. In the absence of anyone in control, I'll be in control. That's my mantra, I stick by it and work at it in everything I do.

You are a leader in your own life and it's really important you accept responsibility for who you are and where you're at. What we know is that leadership can be taught by getting clear on the vision for the business, how you're going to execute that and the team of teams you need to build to make it happen more often.

CHAPTER 60: SIMPLE PRODUCTIVITY HACKS THAT CHANGE THE GAME.

You can skin the onion as much as you want, but eventually, you'll get to the core and it's the most potent because it's what's given the strength to grow the rest. It's the same in your business and life; get clear about where you add the special sauce, the magic that makes it happen and then put the systems and people around you to do the rest; that's called fitness, especially when you and the people around you are fit for their roles.

CHAPTER 61: SHOW ME YOUR CALENDAR, YOUR BANK STATEMENT AND YOUR MOBILE PHONE AND I'LL TELL YOU YOUR PRIORITIES.

Where you spend your time, your money and your attention matters. You can't buy time, but you can increase the quality of it. You can earn money, but your attention needs to be focused on getting you to the summit of your personal Everest.

Here are some productivity hacks that will help you achieve more of your potential.

1. Follow this rule: Do you have to do this and will it help you to get you to where you want to go? If the answer is no to either of those questions, pass it on.
2. Your calendar is everything. Everyone on my team has access to my calendar; even outside consultants have access. I have nothing to hide. I'm a massive planner and I love routine. The most productive people in the world are mums and you'll see that routine sets them free. Work your routine.

– Set your health appointments first. I map out my exercise, personal trainer and meal times. It's all about renewal and health is number one.

– All-day appointments are great for keeping your routine in check. I use these for calls that need to be made on that day. I pair these together with my directions' meeting notes. These are the things I need my team to do for me and essential conversations that need to be had. I write the appointment in my calendar on the fly. That way, I don't have to remember anything because it's always on my calendar.

– Use all-day appointments as agendas. I also use the meetings with my staff as our agendas. I'm not at my best all the time, so I use agendas to jog my memory around the essential questions for each role to ensure progress. When you give your team an agenda for the meeting and it's the same each time, it allows them to prepare for it. Then, I just get them to do the work to work the agenda. They turn up to the meeting like superstars, well-prepared and on-track. I set the expectations high for myself and for those that are around me. If you're not clear on what you want, then how will they be?

– Notes in my iPhone are my saviours. I put everything in there from quotes to key movies I should watch and book recommendations; you name it. Those sync to the cloud, so I never lose anything. Searching is a wonderful thing that lets you find what you want when you need it.

3. Get out of bed early; be an early riser. The easiest way to do that is to go to bed early. I remember being in a nightclub with a mate. He was the DJ and we were in the DJ booth. We looked out over the crowd and I asked him the question, "How many people in here have what we want? How many are earning $1 million a year or more?" We both looked at each other. None. Hang out where the people who you want to be hang out. I like to start early; it sets the intention for the day. If you go to bed early, drink one litre of water just before you got to bed. I guarantee you'll have no problems getting out of bed in the morning and you'll be very focused on the first activity of the day. Then, when you get to the bathroom have all of your gym gear laid out, jump into that and set your appointment with your personal trainer so you have to be there. Show up; it counts.

4. Realise that emotions will get in the way. You will have to fight the resistance. Kill the automatic negative thoughts; we all get them. Emotions come before the actions, yet when you do the actions, they change your emotions. You don't feel like going for a run, but you do the run anyway and then you feel heaps better after the run.

People love people who are doers, people who do what they say they are going to do and people who are enthusiasts at life. Be that person.

"I began to realise how important it was to be an enthusiast in life. He taught me that if you are interested in something, no matter what it is, go at it at full speed ahead. Embrace it with both arms, hug it, love it and above all become passionate about it. Lukewarm is no good. Hot is no good either. White hot and passionate is the only thing to be."
— Roald Dahl

"Go to sleep with a dream, wake up with a purpose." — Unknown

Sometimes, you just want to shake people and wake them up from their haze. Remember the golden rule: People have to want it more than you want it for them. You can show them the way, but it's up to them to pursue that path.

You see it all to often: the loss of a loved one, a divorce, the loss of a child, or a trigger event that either breaks you or makes you. Don't be one of those people that need a trigger event before they get serious about achieving their potential. We all have more than enough time until we don't. Pursue the path to greatness, which is the purpose of life.

"My aim in life isn't so much the pursuit of happiness as the happiness of pursuit." – Charles Saatchi.

CHAPTER 62: SUPERMAN VERSUS SUPER TEAM — THE BIGGER THE DREAM, THE MORE IMPORTANT THE TEAM.

You can do everything yourself for a while until you realise that the only way to do more and achieve more is to get specific about what you want and why you want it. If you want it enough, you'll build a team and do something wonderful. Think about Elon Musk, Henry Ford, Steve Jobs, all of them are creators who have changed human existence as we know it.

CHAPTER 63: ELIMINATE DISTRACTIONS.

We live in the most distracted society that has ever existed. Since the advent of the mobile phone, life has sped up. The speed of life today is the fastest it's ever been and the slowest it will ever be for the rest of your life.

As you get older, you will do more in a day, so make sure you're doing more of what you love doing. I challenge you to remove all social media from your phone just for a month and see what happens to the quality of your life.

Make sure you have your email set to manual so that you have to select send and receive or pull down on the mail on your phone to collect it.

I've turned off the notifications section on my phone. I'll decide when I want to be in the loop and when I want to be out of it. The key here is if this will or won't help me to get where I want to go. If it doesn't help, it goes.

Relationships are the same. I only want to be involved where I can add value, meaning, or fun and laughter. If I'm not feeling it, then neither is the other person. I don't do awkward. I call it if it's awkward.

We've entered a world where time-sucking happens more than you know. How often have you spent thirty minutes on your phone and said, "You know what? That was an awesome thirty minutes of my life. Can I do it again?" It's not often. It's the real experiences that matters, the ones that take your breath away. It's the meaningful ones when we get to connect with those around us, share stories and insights and have that real human connection.

It doesn't matter how many friends you have on social media if you're still at home alone on a Saturday night.

A great business gives you purpose. It allows you to connect with people and be at the highest level of Maslow's hierarchy of needs in problem-solving. The more we help others, the more we help ourselves.

We talk to ourselves more than anyone else talks to us. That's why it's really important to make sure you honour your word and talk positively to yourself. You have to be your own cheerleader. Every time I get scared about doing something that's outside of my comfort zone, that strong, dominating voice comes over the loudspeaker and says, "You will do this. You're capable of more and this right now, it's called growth. Throw yourself into it."

I've found that I work at my best when I'm backed into a corner or have been given a tight timeline. That's when I produce my best work. The secret is to back yourself, do the work that matters and get known for being really, really good at what you do.

That's why I love working in 45-minute sessions. I do lots of things in 45-minute sessions, from call sessions to email clearing to cleaning up at home. Use your time efficiently and remember a reward will follow your efforts. Too many people get the rewards without putting in the necessary effort. Lift heavier weights and you will be stronger.

If you've got unhealthy addictions, seek help. For most of us, our phones fit that criteria. Keep a record of the time you spend on your phone. There's plenty of great apps that will measure what you do on your phone every day. Review the log and see how much of it was really essential.

It is best to strip away the distractions because they can hold you and your business back.

Use time wisely. Will it matter what you're doing on your phone five years from now? What about 20 years from now? Keep things in perspective; it's never as bad as you think it will be, just as it's never as good as you had expected.

Set expectations for yourself and build to uphold those every day. Don't jump on and off. Surging sucks energy and it sucks the life out of you. Build energy in yourself and others. You do that through great meaningful relationships.

CHAPTER 64: BASICS AND EXTRAS.

The truth we all ignore is that we get caught up in the extras. We move to the shiny new before we've even mastered the basics.

Champions are good at the basics. They strip everything to its core. You can't have discipline in one area of your life and not have it in others.

These are the basics on which to focus:
1. Learn. Be open to learning all the time.
2. Deliver. What you ship matters.
3. Calendar. Build a marketing calendar.
4. Plan. Plan well ahead. Plan at least 25 years out, then 5, then the next 12 months, then the next quarter, then the next day and then the next hour. Become a great planner; it helps you stay prepared.
Execute. Be a doer. Do the basics really well. Book the appointments, be a people person who smiles, makes the calls, get in the doors, love what you do and be interested.

CHAPTER 65: BUILD YOUR MOTOR.

I'm amazed at how little progress people really make because they waste their lives away in not making decisions and not building their capacity. Once you've found your system, your way of doing things, you can reach heights of extreme productivity. You realize that it's up to you to build your motor.

This comes down to character. How do you want to be remembered and what for? It combines with your legacy. Here are some character traits I practice every day.

1. Be fun. Laughter unites. Pick your audience, but make it fun to be around you.
2. Be driven. Be clear on what you want. No one is going to decide on it for you. You have to decide on what you want; it's the great asset you'll have and the vision for what you want in your life.
3. Be consistent – annoyingly consistent. If I said I'd do it, consider it done. I don't ride the highs and lows of life anymore; I like to keep it consistent. I've built coping mechanisms for both, so I can smooth them out. When something amazing happens, I'll celebrate it but get straight back to work. When something average happens, I think about what system I could put in place so it doesn't happen again. Then, I say, "It is what it is" and move on quickly.
4. Energetic. Energy matters in business and in life. Your number-one job is to renew it — to bring the best energy to the table at all times. Look after yourself; it matters even in times of high stress. It's what you do when you get busy (and tells us a lot about what you really value). Remember, health comes first, family comes second, business comes third and that's the order in which they go into your diary.
5. Respectful. People will come at you and they will have different

opinions. The great thing is that they are entitled to them. Sometimes, I just think to myself, "That's cool; there goes old mate with his opinions again." The great thing about them is that they don't have to be yours. Everyone is equal in my book; we all desire a better life and have the right to work towards it.

6. Creative. Innovation matters; it's what makes the world a better place. It also makes you a much better negotiator. Get creative with everything you do.

7. Be an all-around good person to be around. Smile, be the life of the party, help people open up and be a chief confidence builder. These will do wonders for your business.

When you know how to behave, you act that way all the time. I just think about if my future self will be happy with today's decisions.

CHAPTER 66: IF YOU MET YOURSELF FROM 10 YEARS AGO, WHAT WOULD YOUR ADVICE BE TO YOURSELF FROM 10 YEARS AGO?

This one question just keeps coming up and it's worth answering. The older you get, the sooner you realise that you wish you had known what's in this book a lot earlier. Reading a book is not hard, but reading the right one at the right time comes down to selection. There's a reason this book found you and you found it. It's because in ten years, you'll wish that you had done more with what you had. We over anticipate what we can get done in a day but significantly underachieve on what we can get done in our lifetimes. Be a goal digger, drive with your ambition, put a stake in the ground and go out there and reach your potential.

Phil Knight, the founder of Nike, said it best in his book *Shoe Dog:* "You measure yourself, by the number of people that measure themselves by you." Remember that you have everything you'll ever need to achieve your potential and if you don't, that's okay because the purpose is strong inside of you and you'll find a way. I hope one day to meet you and hear just how much you've done in growing your capacity and biting off more of your potential.

Questions for change:

- What do you want?
- Why are you here?
- What are you capable of?

- Why are you not there?
- What needs to change?
- Are you prepared to pay what it costs?
- Are you prepared to make the change?
- Where will you be in 5 years?
- Where will you be in 25 years? That's more important.
- Who will be there with you?
- What have you experienced?
- Have you set yourself up for success? If not, why not?
- When are you at your best?

CHAPTER 67: THE CREED.

You deserve success. It starts with every step you take. It continues with what you do each day to achieve your true potential.

It requires you to be clear on what success looks like to you.

You need to believe and then you need to execute your belief with precision.

Happiness comes from within. It survives by shaping your environment and teaching people how to use your time.

Today, how will you invest your energy?

Who can open more doors for you today?

How do you get a bigger audience?

Decide what you really want and really go for it.

You've got one chance at the life you deserve.

Hard work, determination and attitude are everything.

Make sure the people around you inspire the hell out of you.

You want people in your life who push you way beyond what you're capable of.

Expand, chase, hunt and grow for what really stimulates the real you.

Authenticity is not something you can fake. Realness comes from knowing who you are and what you are about.

Cherish opportunities but leave behind the negatives.

Find the edge and stay out on it more often. It's much more exciting.

Don't get caught up in the image; just be who you are at your core.

It's much too big a world and you're much too small to be worried about if you can do something. Just get in there and give it a go.

CHAPTER 68: THE CYCLE OF COMPLETION.

The great thing about life is that when you think you've got everything worked out, when everything is perfect, something changes and needs your attention. It's called the cycle of completion because when you implement your vision, you get more ambitious and things change.

That's what makes you dynamic, constantly working in a changing world and adapting to it. Balance is ever-elusive and you can't avoid problems forever. As Tom Peters puts it, it's either "Wow" or "Not wow." That's it.

So, be hard on yourself and hold yourself to high standards. It lets you hold others to high standards as well.

Life is growth; experiences matter and so do the people that share them with you.

CHAPTER 69: THE FINAL CHAPTER . . . FOR NOW.

In this short book, you've got everything you need to develop a bolder, bigger vision; no one came here to play it small. Bite more than you can chew and then find a way to chew it.

Grow your skills and get fit in business and every other area of your life by constantly working away at it. Next, build the systems, the way of doing things that get you the desired results and then scale with great people. No one makes it on one's own.

The big lessons are the ones that grow you the most. The more you try, the more you fail and the more you fail, the quicker you learn. What I've learnt so far is that the bigger your dream is, the faster you build your team. You find a way. As you grind away at your potential, you find new ways to open up capacity. Every time you do that, you open up new ideas for growing your potential.

You will never be done. There will be more work. You are capable of more and with this one approach to fitness, systems and people, anything is possible. If you do it right, you'll learn to love the journey. You'll get uncomfortable and wish in 10 years time that you had backed yourself in more, done it earlier and played full on and all out.

I wish you well. Connect, share and make life great. Join the movement. Email josh@joshphegan.com.au and share your story.

Josh Phegan.

ABOUT THE AUTHOR

Josh Phegan is the internationally renowned go-to speaker, trainer and coach for high-performance real estate agents and agencies. He is the number one preferred trainer for Australia's top 100 agents and top 50 women in real estate.

In 2016 he took his career to a new level, speaking at more than 208 events in the US, UK, New Zealand and Australia. His mission is to inspire agents to achieve their potential and financial freedom.

He personally coaches some of the who's who in the real estate industry, both new, emerging and high-performance agents, with his number one sales agent writing in excess of $8.75m in fees, with over 196 transactions.

He hosts industry-leading events such as the Real Estate BluePrint and List Sell Negotiate, is the producer behind the high performance podcast with Alexander Phillips.

To rapidly help his clients achieve their potential he has built a unique online training platform to measure and track the numbers that count for soft and hard KPIs, together with access to every piece of training content he has ever produced. In a way, Josh has automated the role of a great sales manager to monitor what counts and help lift agents up.

His company's digital products and marketing have received top accolades internationally, helping to drive huge growth in his business.

Josh works with leading real estate agencies at both training and boardroom levels. Individually, he works with brand new people to help them establish the critical skills and behaviours to rapidly drive their careers and with industry heavyweight agents who have achieved incredible results of up to 196+ transactions per year.

He is often in boardrooms providing strategic direction and support for fast growth companies, with his fastest client scaling from 0-19 offices in under six years.

FURTHER READING.

Books we think you will enjoy:

- *The Power of Full Engagement* by Tony Schwartz, James E. Loehr
- *The Checklist Manifesto* by Atul Gawande
- *Shoe Dog* by Phil Knight
- *The Magic of Thinking Big* by David J. Schwartz
- *Being Mortal* by Atul Gawande
- *Mastering The Rockerfeller Habits* by Verne Harnish

Made in the USA
Columbia, SC
17 July 2017